WEAVING BIG on a LITTLE LOOM

WEAVING BIG on a LITTLE LOOM

CREATE INSPIRED LARGER PIECES

Fiona Daly

PRINCETON ARCHITECTURAL PRESS · NEW YORK

Published by
Princeton Architectural Press
70 West 36th Street, 11th Floor
New York, NY 10018
www.papress.com

Conceived, edited, and designed by
Quarto Publishing plc
an imprint of The Quarto Group
6 Blundell Street
London N7 9BH
www.quarto.com

Princeton Architectural Press edition, 2022

Printed and bound in Singapore
25 24 23 22 4 3 2 1

ISBN: 978-1-64896-122-9

For Quarto:
Editor: Jenny Fox-Proverbs
Projects editor: Anna Galkina
Designer: Rachel Cross
Photographers: Al Higgins, Nicki Dowey, and Phil Wilkins
Illustrator: Kuo Kang Chen
Art director: Gemma Wilson
Publisher: Lorraine Dickey

For Princeton Architectural Press:
Editors: Rob Shaeffer and Stephanie Holstein
Cover Design: Paul Wagner

Special thanks to Cynthia Alberto of The Weaving Hand, Gretchen Jaeger of Halcyon Yarns, and Karen Gerstel of Under Mountain Weavers for their invaluable feedback.

Library of Congress Control Number: 2021948960

CONTENTS

MEET FIONA

Hello! My name is Fiona Daly and I'm a textile designer-maker, handweaver, and writer from Ireland. My practice is craft- and research-led, focusing on sustainable textiles, circular design, weave, and education. I am a member of Design & Crafts Council Ireland. I design for mills, teach within higher and further education, and run private workshops, while also developing my own handweaving craft practice. I am incredibly passionate about the craft of handweaving, and thoroughly enjoy sharing this love through my teaching and my books. My first book, *Weaving on a Little Loom,* was published in 2018.

My love of constructed textiles began at an early age, influenced by my grandmother, who worked as a lacemaker and ran her own craft shop in the west of Ireland. It was a natural progression that I went on to study Textile Design at the National College of Art & Design in Ireland. During these highly creative, stimulating years, I also had the opportunity to study in Bergen, Norway, where my appreciation of traditional crafts and materials grew. After graduating, I honed my weaving skills while working for a handweaver in the west of Ireland.

Since then, my weaving journey has evolved into many strands. Through weaving residencies in the Shetland Islands and rural Denmark, I greatly developed my woven design skills. During my years in Edinburgh, I was involved in a multidisciplinary craft workshop, where I began teaching weaving courses and fell in love with it! More recently, I went back to school to study for my masters in Textile Design at Chelsea College of Art & Design in London, choosing to study there as it consolidated my interest in sustainable textiles. This allowed me focused time to research core theories and design principles, which now underpin my weaving practice, and which I aim to extend and share more widely through this book.

Slow, sustainable, and ethical textiles are all striving toward the same aspirational goal—a healthier relationship between us, our clothes and textiles, and our planet. A "slow movement" means just that—to slow down speed—and it can be applied to just about anything. The concept is born out of the Slow Food movement, the brainchild of Carlo Petrini, with roots dating back to 1986 in Italy. It aims to celebrate regional, local cuisine, made from well-sourced, quality ingredients. Thanks to Carl Honoré's book *In Praise of Slow* (2004), the "slow movement" concept has mushroomed globally, encompassing industries as broad as food, design, and agriculture, among many more.

The Slow Textiles movement developed as a response to the twentieth-century's detrimental fast fashion industry of mass-produced clothing, with its ill-considered materials, production, and supply chains. In contrast, slow design encourages designers to make a conscientious choice when it comes to materials and processes. At the same time, it urges designers and consumers alike to slow down the ever-increasing pace of fashion and textiles.

The philosophies behind the Fibershed movement borrow from this "slow" framework. Established by the pioneering Rebecca Burgess, Fibershed urges us to ask the same questions of our clothing as we now do of our food. A "fibershed" can be described as a geographical landscape that provides

the resources and infrastructure to create a local, regional textile supply chain with low environmental impact. Meanwhile, sustainable textiles represent the need to improve the sustainability of the textiles throughout their life cycle, from design to end of use.

Throughout the process of writing this book and designing its projects, I have kept these principles in mind. In the first chapter, you will find a section on the origin of materials, linking you, the weaver, back to the beginnings of your yarns. The yarn suppliers carefully selected for the project designs all share my local, ethical, and sustainable ethos.

As my weaving practice is rooted in sustainable design ethos, I wanted to feed this approach into the book, and share these ideas with other weavers. My aim is to encourage you, the hobbyist weaver, to consider your choice of materials and their environmental impact. Throughout the book there is an underlying focus on encouraging weavers to use sustainable, locally produced yarns and materials.

Being restricted by the size of the loom, particularly a frame loom, is a frustration I hear so often from my students, especially when they are in their weaving groove. So in this book, I also wish to encourage you to push your frame loom to its limits to weave long textile pieces, something that you may not have considered before! Through weaving the projects in this book, it is my hope that you will create your own slow textiles—a collection of large textiles for you and your home, from bags to an oversized scarf to pillows. Through thinking a bit about these concepts, I also hope the growing conversation around sustainable textiles can be explored in your own patch of the weaving world.

Happy Weaving!

Fiona

CHAPTER 1

MATERIAL CHOICES

TEXTILES AND THE ENVIRONMENT

For me, Fall 2018 marked a turning point in public awareness of the pressing issue of climate emergency. October 2018 saw the publication of the landmark report by United Nations body the Intergovernmental Panel on Climate Change. Shortly after, in December 2018, Sir David Attenborough attended the opening of the 24th UN Climate Change Conference (COP24) in Poland. Delivering the People's Seat Address, he advocated passionately for the need by everyone to take action. Greta Thunberg's ongoing School Strike for Climate Change, and Extinction Rebellion's protests, were set to the backdrop of the horrific impacts of raging bush fires, flash floods, earthquakes, and droughts being experienced around the globe today. We were warned of such catastrophic events, but they are still shocking to observe and devastating to experience.

The Role of Weaving

What has all this to do with handweaving? Weaving is the craft of creating textiles. At this moment, of all industries across the world, the fashion and textiles industry is the second largest pollutant. This is largely a result of the twentieth-century invention of the detrimental fast fashion model. According to the Ellen McArthur Foundation, the production of textiles produces over one billion tons of greenhouse gas emissions of CO_2 equivalent per year—more than international flights and shipping combined. The UN estimates that almost 10 percent of total global emissions come from the fashion and textiles industry.

Beyond the emissions, the textiles industry is responsible for negative environmental impact in many more ways. Dyes made of toxic chemicals leak into our waterways resulting in water pollution. Polyesters shed plastic microfibers in domestic washing machines, which end up in drinking water and aquatic food chains, eventually consumed by humans. Cotton, a very popular natural fiber, takes vast amounts of water to grow—approximately 600,000 gal (2,700 L) of water are needed to grow enough cotton for one t-shirt. This is the equivalent of two-and-a-half years' worth of drinking water for one person.

Consumer Behavior

The impact of all these production processes is scaled up by overconsumption, which is driven by our demand and expectations as consumers. Fast fashion with its linear system—take, make, waste—results in the cheaper monetary cost and lower quality of clothing. It is now cheaper to buy new than to repair. According to the U.S. Environmental Protection Agency's Office of Solid Waste, Americans throw away more than sixty-eight pounds (approx. 30 kg) of clothing and textiles per person each year. Since the early 2000s, fashion production has doubled. Synthetic fibers, which are produced from fossil fuels such as oil and gas, account for 69 percent of all materials used in textiles. This is expected to increase to 75 percent by 2030.

According to the Changing Markets Foundation's report, "Synthetics Anonymous," it is fast fashion's addiction to fossil fuels which is causing this waste crisis. While some major fashion brands are moving toward a more climate conscious approach, greenwashing is rampant. For textiles that fall under the "ocean plastic" banner, the amount of "ocean plastic" used to produce such products is tiny compared to the volume of new plastic used. And it still results in microplastics shedding into our water and food streams.

What We Can Do Now

Natural fibers such as those used in this book are extracted from plants and shorn from animals. Making textiles from natural fibers, preferably undyed or naturally dyed, has lower environmental impact. Among the benefits are that all can be fully composted when no longer usable and thus complete the soil-to-soil cycle. While the debate is not black and white and natural fibers do not always have a squeaky-

Naturally dyed yarn displayed at a market stall in Peru.

clean supply chain, I feel a move toward 100 percent natural fibers is the most sensible. Natural fibers have been in use for textile production for millennia to clothe us and furnish our homes, without harming our planet. In my opinion, we need to end the reliance on drilling oil for fiber production, and to go further than recycling materials in order to achieve the circular model the fashion and textiles industry needs to adopt. For me, the best future of textiles lies in an industry based on natural fibers that can be grown regeneratively and returned to the soil in a climate-positive way.

I feel our choice of yarns and fibers, however small, can have an impact on our natural environment and contribute toward making a more sustainable textiles industry.

FURTHER READING

If you'd like to delve a little deeper into initiatives for the future of sustainability in the textiles industry, I'd recommend these sources to begin with:

- Ellen McArthur Foundation
  ellenmacarthurfoundation.org
- UN Alliance for Sustainable Fashion
  unfashionalliance.org
- WRAP UK
  wrap.org.uk
- Changing Markets Foundation
  changingmarkets.org

THE ORIGIN OF MATERIALS

"The soil that feeds us is also the soil that clothes us."

Fibershed: Growing a Movement of Farmers, Fashion Activists, and Makers for a New Textile Economy, Rebecca Burgess (2019)

Because of their lower environmental impact, I focus on the use of natural fibers, as opposed to man-made (synthetic) fibers. Natural fibers can be grown and harvested in sustainable ways, making them renewable. In addition, they can be grown regeneratively, so that they contribute to the soil in a climate-positive way. Among the benefits of using natural fibers are their high absorbency, durability, and their ability to fully biodegrade at the end of their life cycle.

Natural fibers can be broken into two main categories: animal and plant. Animal fibers grow externally on the animal and include fleece, hair, down, and fur. They can all be shorn without harming the living animal, and because the fibers regrow, they are a renewable resource. Plant fibers are extracted from many parts of the plant, generally the stalks and leaves. Working with natural fibers connects us to the earth and builds upon the heritage of those that came before us.

The fibers showcased in this section are biosphere-based fibers of sheep and alpaca wool, as well as fibers from hemp, flax, and nettle plants. These fibers make up the yarns used in the projects, chosen for their sustainable and natural qualities. All of these fibers can be found in the northern hemisphere and beyond. It has been my intention in choosing these fibers that they are readily available locally to you, wherever you are in the world. It is my hope that knowing a little more about the source of each of these wonderful fibers will encourage you to seek out natural fibers and experiment in the future.

SHEEP'S WOOL

Sheep are thought to have been domesticated by humans eight to ten thousand years ago (the first animal after the dog!) and have been providing us with fiber for clothing and our dwellings ever since. Originating in the Middle East, sheep migrated through North Africa, Europe, and beyond. The first sheep were multicolored animals. According to the Greek legend of the Golden Fleece, some early selection in sheep breeding occurred to create whiter fleeces. Ancients Romans were instrumental in the migration of sheep and shepherding skills, and the original stock for the merino sheep in Spain is thought to have developed from these flocks.

In Britain, spinning and weaving developed around 1900 BCE. The first native sheep derived from wild sheep similar to today's Soay breed, and the British wool industry had already been established by the time of the Roman invasion in 55 BCE. With this, further refinement of breeding selection ensued, as did with the Viking and later Norman sheep additions. By the twelfth century, Britain was the heart of the global wool industry, which in turn was central to the British economy. Innovations to speed up its production, such as weaving mills, spurred on the British Industrial Revolution in the eighteenth century. Today, sheep are still found on farms all over the world, with the largest number found in China (143 million), followed by Australia (98 million). Although Britain's flock has considerably fewer sheep (25 million), it still retains the largest number of individual breeds, each of which carry varying properties.

The fleece is shorn from the sheep annually for many years, making it a sustainable, renewable fiber. The fiber itself is hollow and cylindrical with scales, and it is these scales that give wool its unique insulating properties. Wool is extremely versatile and used for many applications, from fashion and textiles, to rope, and house insulation.

PROPERTIES

- **Warm and insulating:** Wool is the original fiber for warmth.
- **Durable:** Extremely hardwearing, wool can withstand wear and tear over a long period.
- **Stretch:** Wool has great elasticity.
- **Naturally flame retardant:** Wool is self-extinguishing. Untreated wool can withstand temperatures up to 1,058°F (570°C).
- **Water absorbent:** Wool can absorb 33 percent of its own weight in water, this resistance makes it very suitable for northern climates.
- **Temperature regulator:** Wool will react to its environment or wearer.
- **Static resistant:** Unlike synthetics, this resistance makes it more suitable for high safety environments such as cars, planes, and trains.

LINEN

Linen is a bast fiber, coming from the stalk of the flax plant. It is an historic textile, with its earliest written mention on tablets from Ancient Greece dating from four thousand years ago. Linen production thrived in Northern Europe, with flax's ability to grow in cool climates and its quick-drying properties. It was later brought to North America with farming settlers. However, the development of the cotton industry pushed flax and linen skills aside until more recent years. During the linen boom of the Victorian era, Ireland was at the heart of the linen industry in Europe.

Flax is a tall, thin plant that grows on a hundred-day cycle, and is planted annually. It has fine, spear-shaped leaves, and its long, straight, and smooth fibers result in a textile which is durable and has a beautiful drape. The process of extracting the fibers from the stalk begins with retting—submersing the stalks in water to stimulate bacterial growth, softening the fibers. After this, the stalks go through stages known as breaking, scutching, and hackling—releasing the fibers within for spinning into yarn.

PROPERTIES

- **Stiff:** Linen fiber has "memory" and retains shape.
- **Cooling:** Linen is suitable for summer wear.
- **Very strong:** Like all plant fibers, linen is stronger when wet, and so is particularly suitable for purposes such as dish cloths, shower scrubbers, or muslins for straining food.
- Breathable
- Light
- Absorbent
- Quick-drying

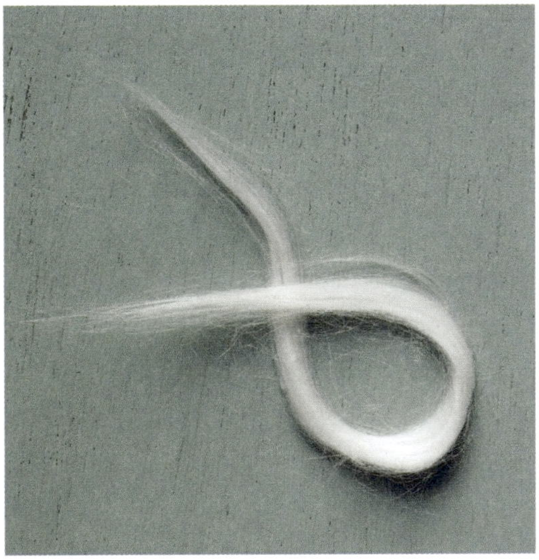

NETTLE

Nettle is a lustrous, bast fiber, whose use in textile production dates back to the Bronze Age in Europe. The fibers are white and silky and can be up to two inches (5 cm) in length. Stronger than linen, especially when wet, it can also be finer than linen and even as fine as cotton; yet, it is stiffer. The process to separate the fiber from the stalk is similar to that of hemp and flax, involving processes called breaking, scutching, and hackling. From here, the nettle fiber can be spun into yarn.

Nettle species grow all over the world and all can be used in textile production. Stinging nettle (*Urtica dioica*), Ramie (*Boehmeria nivea*), and Himalayan nettle (*Girardinia diversifolia*) are the most commonly used in textiles. They can grow easily and in abundance in varying habitats. The sting comes from barbs on the leaves (which disappear when cooked) and so nettle textiles have no sting. During the two world wars, nettle fiber was used as a replacement for cotton for clothing and army uniforms, due to shortages. A large advantage of nettle-fiber production, and an area of continued research, is that it requires less water than cotton. It could become a great substitute for cotton as a sustainable crop in the future.

PROPERTIES

- **Longevity:** Nettle has the longest lifespan of all natural fibers.
- Light weight
- Quick drying and resistant to mildew
- Lustrous
- Very little elasticity and therefore very strong

ALPACA

Alpacas, along with llamas, are part of the Camelid family and originate in the South American countries of Peru, Chile, and Bolivia. The domestication of the alpaca began five thousand years ago in the Inca Empire, and its fiber has been in use for textiles ever since. The Spanish invasion of South America in the sixteenth century brought the alpaca to Europe. It also brought merino sheep to South America, causing havoc with the Inca's excellent breeding system developed for fiber quality. Despite this, alpaca fiber is still considered one of the most luxurious of natural fibers. Queen Victoria is reputed to have worn dresses of alpaca fiber.

There are two varieties of alpaca—the huacaya and the suri—and both produce fiber. The huacaya is much more common, making up 90 to 93 percent of the population, and is the fiber you are more likely to use. Exclusively alpaca yarns are rare to find, as the fiber is often mixed with a small percentage of sheep's wool to ease the spinning process and add elasticity. Today, alpaca are farmed not only in South America and Europe, but also North America, Canada, New Zealand, and Australia.

PROPERTIES

- Natural crimp
- Dense
- Bright
- Very soft
- Excellent drape
- Twenty-two natural shades
- Insulating properties
- Hypoallergenic

HEMP

Hemp (*Cannabis sativa*) is thought to be one of the oldest cultivated plants in the world, dating back to 8000 BCE, and has been found the world over. It continued to be a popular agricultural crop until the 1920s. Hemp fiber was widely used for rope, paper, clothing, home furnishings, sails, shoes, and more. As hemp (sometimes called industrial hemp) is part of the Cannabaceae family, it fell under new drug acts and became illegal to cultivate. Despite industrial hemp not containing high concentrations of tetrahydrocannabinol (THC)—as found in marijuana—it was included in these bills, much to the detriment of the hemp textile industry.

As brands and designers seek more sustainable materials, hemp fiber is once again growing in popularity today. It is a bast fiber, like flax, yet it requires specialist technology to separate the fiber from the woody part of the stalk, or hurd, in a process known as retting. It is a high-yield, low-input crop, averaging a yield of two tons per acre (18,000 kg per 4 sq. km). With a hundred-day growing cycle, it grows tall quickly—some varieties can grow up to 15 ft. (4.5 m) tall.

PROPERTIES

- Yields 250 percent more fiber than cotton and 600 percent more fiber than flax on the same amount of land.
- Strong
- Durable
- Long fibers
- High-yield, low-input crop

SUSTAINABLE YARN CHOICES

As a designer and weaver, I feel I have an environmental responsibility for my choice of material, and I would like to extend that philosophy to everyone whose hands this book ends up in. As crafters and weavers in the twenty-first century, it is our duty to scratch the surface a little deeper and ask questions about the provenance of the materials we choose to use. Borrowing from the successful Who Made My Clothes? movement, apply the same thinking to your weaving by asking yourself: Who made my yarn?

Among the suggested ways of reducing our fashion and textile impacts are buying secondhand and shopping local. This section looks at ways to do both. Through buying secondhand, we are extending the life cycle of a garment or textile and not contributing to new production. By shopping local, the environmental cost of shipping and packaging is reduced, and we're supporting a local economy. View it similarly to how you might think of your food—would you prefer to eat tomatoes grown on the opposite side of the globe, or grown in the neighboring county? Of course, consuming less can also reduce our impacts. Limiting your yarn stash may encourage you to choose wisely and make consciously considered choices.

Taking Fibershed's framework as a guide, key things to consider when sourcing your yarns are:

- **Source:** What is the raw material and where does it come from?
- **Transparency:** How and where is it converted into yarn?
- **Connectivity:** How are all these key stages connected, from the soil to your hands as a maker to eventually returning to soil?

As we know from the previous section, natural textile fibers can come from both plants and animals. So, begin by considering which animals and plants are local to your country or region, and therefore which yarns it would be possible to make locally. Look for suppliers who can tell you about, or even better show you, their supply chain and provenance of their material. Perhaps you can visit a local farm to meet the sheep who grew the wool for the yarns you wish to purchase from their farm shop? Can you trace the wool's journey from farm to mill? Whose hands did it pass through before it reached yours? Connecting with your yarn's journey will help you add value to it and ultimately increase its longevity. The yarns used in the projects in this book were selected with this framework in mind. Despite working on varying scales, all the yarn suppliers share this same ethos.

REUSING & REPURPOSING YARNS

A generation or two ago, it was quite a common sight for old sweaters to be unraveled and then reknit to create a new version. My mother remembers quite clearly assisting my grandmother in the process of unraveling and winding skeins and balls. Similar to repair skills, these skills are almost lost today. The notion of unpicking a textile just to create another may seem odd to some. But similar to the concept that the most sustainable clothing you can have are the clothes already in your closet, the most sustainable yarns you can use are the ones you already own. I invite you to look at your closet and soft furnishings with fresh eyes. Perhaps you have a sweater or blanket you love the feel of, but it is worn in patches—could this be given a new lease on life as a scarf, perhaps?

By repurposing old yarns, the life cycle of the garment or textile is extended and waste is reduced. Buying secondhand from your local thrift store is another great way of gathering new-to-you yarns, while not contributing to new textile production. One of the projects in this book, the Tote Bag (see page 92), showcases repurposed yarns from my local thrift store. With this project, my aim is to inspire you to further develop your own projects using repurposed yarns. The sequence below shows you how to unpick a knit garment in order to repurpose the yarn.

Calculating Length of Your Yarn

1. Before unraveling your chosen textile or garment, remove any buttons, hardware, or labels, then weigh it to check the total weight.

2. After unraveling the yarn and winding it into a ball (see below), weigh it again. Measure out 10 yd. (9 m) of yarn and weigh this. Calculate the total meterage of yarn based on the total weight using the following calculation:

$$\frac{\text{total weight}}{\text{10 yd. (9 m) weight}} \times 10\ (9) = \text{total yardage (meterage)}$$

Calculating Weight of Your Yarn

To determine whether the weight of a repurposed yarn is suitable for the intended weaving project, measure its e.p.i. (ends per inch), as explained in "Dressing the Loom" (see page 26).

If you think the e.p.i. is too high for your project, try doubling up the yarn, winding two strands in the place of one.

Unpicking a Knit Garment

1. Begin by using a stitch ripper to remove any stitched or linked seams. This will include not only side and piece seams, but also any cuffs or collars, which are made from separate pieces.

2. Next, identify in which direction the piece was knit, as you will need to find the last few stitches made. Most often, knit tops and sweaters are knit from the bottom up. Most probably, the end will be near the shoulders on one side of the garment, such as in the piece in the image.

3. Make a snip here and pull the yarn. When pulling from the end of the knitting, the yarn will pull away easily, row by row. If it does not, try unraveling from the other end of the garment.

4. Lay the garment flat (on your lap) and then pull the yarn. The loops of the previous knit row of stitches will be visible. Wind into a tight ball as you unravel.

CHAPTER 2

TOOLS & TECHNIQUES

ALL ABOUT THE LOOM

A loom is any device that holds warp threads taut so that they can be woven. The frame loom used in this book is a basic, low-tech loom in comparison to its loom cousins. It consists of a frame with measured increments across the top and base bars. Warp (vertical) threads are wound tightly and spaced evenly on the frame, in order for weft (horizontal) threads to be woven across them. When weaving on a frame loom, the weft is most often wound around a tool, called a stick shuttle.

The type of frame loom used in this book, however, is more developed than one might think upon first glance. Because the top bar (the warp beam) and base bar (the cloth beam) are detachable and also rotate, it is possible to dress (prepare) the loom with a warp longer than the height of the frame loom itself. In comparison, on a frame loom with static beams, we achieve a "fixed warp," the length of which can only ever be the height of the frame loom. These detachable beams, secured with wing nuts, allow the frame loom weaver to create longer, bigger, and more ambitious projects than one might have considered before. This low-tech weaving gives a great taste for weaving rotating warps on more advanced looms, such as rigid heddle, table, or floor looms. The addition of a heddle bar on this type of frame loom also makes the loom more sophisticated. Using a frame loom in this way is a very accessible introduction to more advanced weaving and can grow your skills and satisfaction as a weaver.

Your weaving equipment and available space are often constraints weavers come up against. For a budding weaver, I recommend this frame loom as it's so neat in size (it is also known as a "lap loom") while also giving you hands-on experience. Your hobby doesn't need to take up your entire living room! In addition, it is so portable that you can easily take your weaving out with you to meet up with other weavers or to weave outdoors.

Another advantage of this type of frame loom is how easily the tension of the warp can be adjusted. Often, after weaving on a warp for a long period of time, the threads tire. They can become either too loose, or if you are nearing the end of the warp, the threads can become frustratingly tight, making it difficult to pass the weft. As the beams can rotate, it is very simple to adjust the tension of the warp threads with a simple twist.

Know Your Loom

Refer to the labels in the photograph opposite and familiarize yourself with all the different parts of the loom.

1. Warp
2. Weft
3. Shuttle
4. Warp beam
5. Cloth beam
6. Wing nut
7. Heddle bar

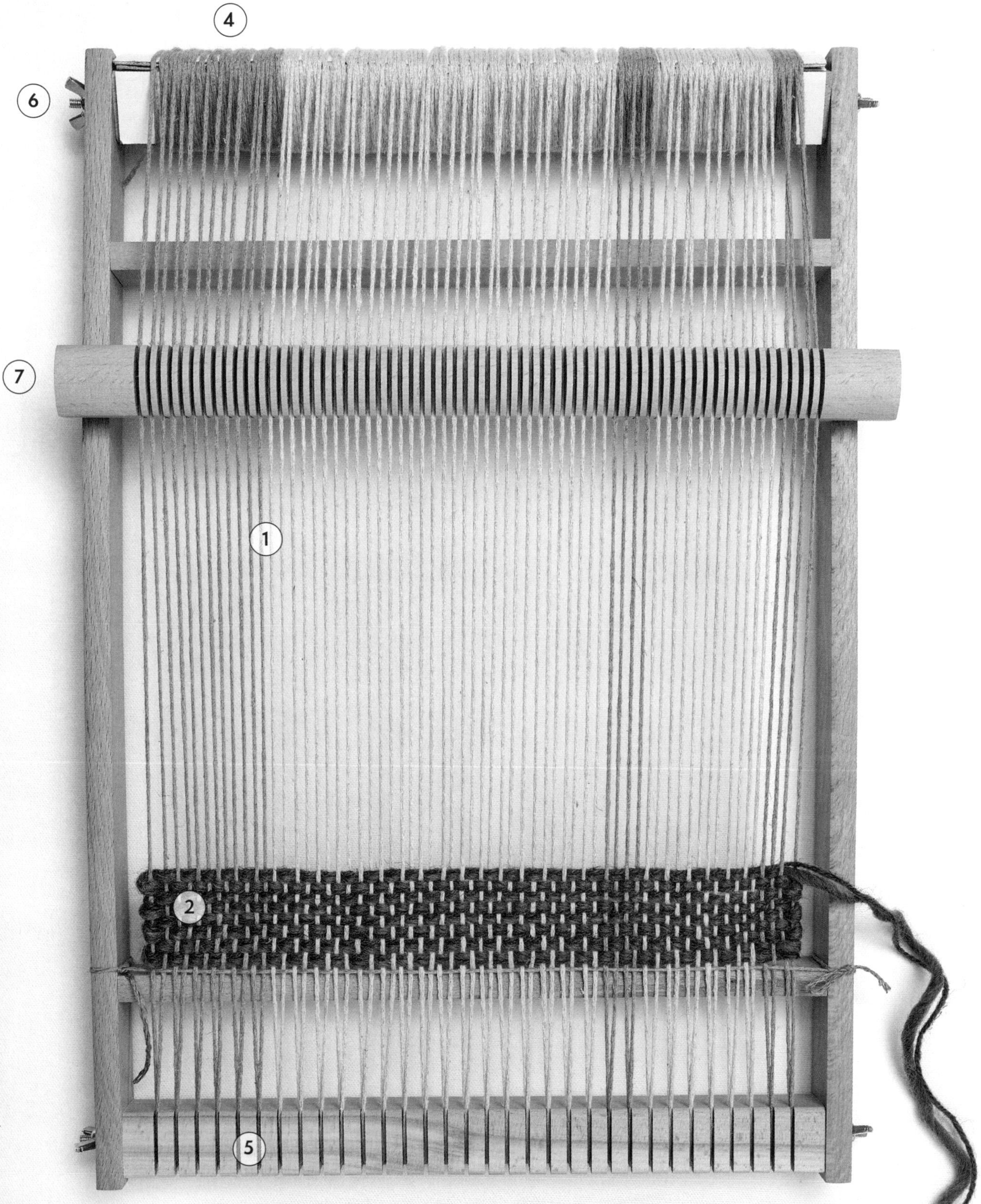
4
6
7
1
2
5
3

MEET THE TOOLS

Here are the tools that you will find most useful when weaving on a frame loom, and will learn how to use in this book.

1 & 2. Stick Shuttle
A stick shuttle is flat, rectangular, and notched at either end. The shuttle is used to hold a length of weft yarn as you pass it through the warp threads. It works best if it is longer than the width of the warp. Many varieties are available.

3. Shed Stick
A shed stick is used to select and lift particular warp threads and, when turned on its edge, provides a shed (opening) when weaving.

4. Pick-up Stick
Used for the same purpose as a shed stick, the pointed tip on this stick allows for ease of selecting and picking up warp threads. It is particularly useful when weaving warp-manipulated weaves, such as leno weave (see page 46) and other patterned weave structures.

5. Heddle Bar
The rotating heddle bar helps to speed up weaving in plain weave structure. It raises alternate warp threads, thus creating an opening (weaving shed) between the warp threads.

6. Weaving Comb
Weaving combs are used to beat down the weft after each row of weaving. They are available in a range of different styles and sizes.

7. Fork Beater
Rather than purchasing a special weaving comb, you can use a kitchen fork to beat down the weft threads while weaving, if you prefer.

8. Tapestry Bobbin
Tapestry bobbins are small spools that are wound with weft yarn and used like a shuttle. They are useful for small areas of weaving, especially if combining sections of different wefts. The pointed end of a bobbin can be used to pick up warp threads and to beat the weft down tightly.

9. Rod
A rod is a very useful weaving tool. It can be used for extra-weft techniques, such as looping, as well as being used as a hanging device. A rod can easily be made from a piece of dowel.

10. Darning Needle
This is a long, blunt needle with a large eye, making it easier to thread with yarn. Darning needles and bodkins are used for finishing a piece of weaving with edging techniques such as hemstitching, fringing, and knot-and-darn edging.

11. Nålbinding Needle
A long, flat, wooden needle with a large eye. It is used as the darning needle and is very suitable for frame loom weaving, especially when working with chunky yarns. It can also be used to weave across the warp. The name comes from a traditional Scandinavian technique.

12. Tape Measure

13. Ruler

14. Scissors

15. Masking Tape

15
12
14
9
5
2
6
10
8
11
7
4
13
1
3

DRESSING THE LOOM

Before starting to weave, you should first plan your project. In chapter one, we discussed material choice and sourcing your yarn in an environmentally and ethically conscious way.

CREATIVE QUESTIONS

Considerations when planning your project should include:

- What is the end piece?
- What is its function?
- Which fiber is most appropriate?
- Which colors and techniques do you wish to use?
- What are the desired finished dimensions?

After answering these questions and arriving at your yarn choice, you can go on to plan your warp.

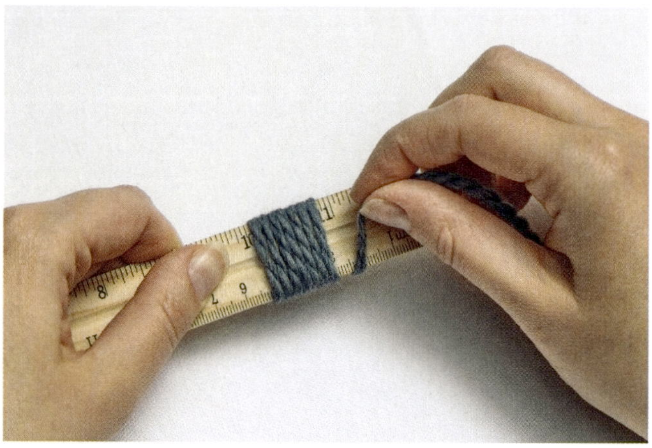

Calculating the Ends Per Inch (e.p.i.)
Use a ruler to calculate the e.p.i. of your yarn.

Calculating the Sett
As yarns vary in thickness, referred to as "weight," they will be dressed accordingly on the loom, as well as according to the desired results. The "sett" of a warp refers to how tightly or narrowly spaced the warp threads are. This is measured by counting the "ends per inch" (e.p.i.), or the number of warp threads in every 1 in. (2.5 cm).

The simplest way to determine the sett of a yarn is to wrap it tightly around a ruler for 1 in. (2.5 cm). Count the number of wraps and then divide this by two to give your total sett.

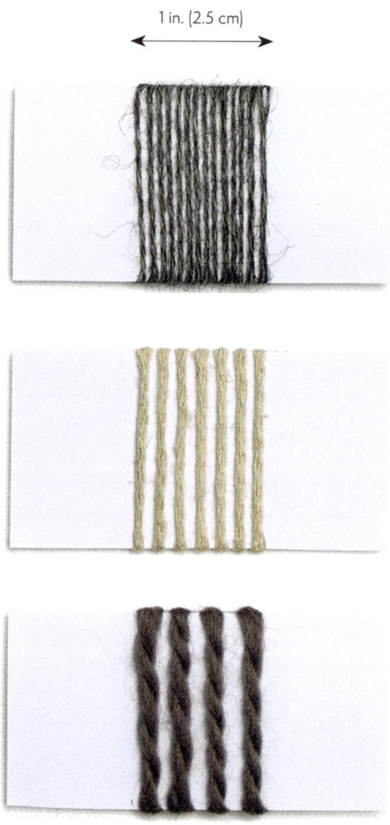

Yarn Weight Comparisons
Here are three examples of yarns in a variety of thicknesses, wrapped over one inch (2.5 cm) of card. Note how the thicker yarn has fewer e.p.i., and therefore a lower sett, than the finest yarn, which has more e.p.i. and thus a higher sett.

Planning the Warp

Now that you have chosen your yarn and calculated the sett using the e.p.i., you can go on to plan the warp in more detail.

Make a note of the following calculations:

- **Warp width:** desired width of project
- **Sett:** e.p.i. divided by two, as explained opposite
- **Total warp ends:** warp width x sett
- **Warp length:** desired project length + take-up (approximately 10 percent) + shrinkage (approximately 10 percent)
- **Total warp yarn needed:** total warp ends x warp length

Once you have all these details for your warp plan, the next step is to dress (prepare) the loom with the warp. This type of frame loom can be dressed in different ways, depending on what you are weaving and how you choose to weave it. The following pages give instructions on how to dress the loom with a fixed (short) warp and a rotating (long) warp, using the heddle bar.

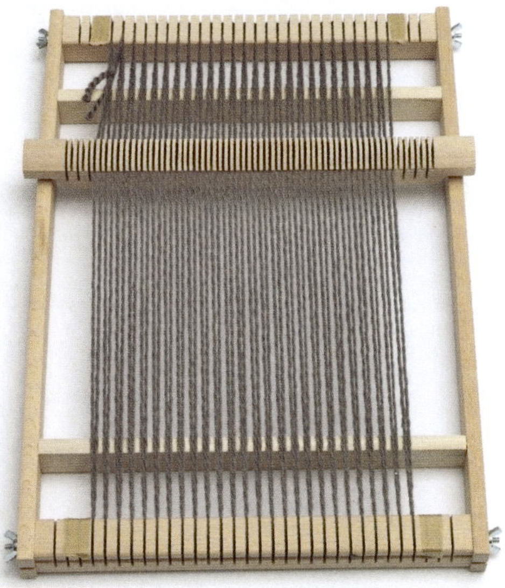

Frame Loom with a Fixed Warp
This loom is dressed with a fixed (short) warp. This means a warp that does not rotate and its maximum length is the height of the frame loom.

Frame Loom with a Rotating (Long) Warp
This loom is dressed with a warp longer than the height of the frame loom, as the top (warp beam) bar and the base (cloth beam) bar rotate.

PREPARING A FIXED (SHORT) WARP

Once on the loom, a fixed warp does not move. The maximum length of a fixed warp is determined by the size of the frame. Typically, three-quarters of the frame height can be woven on a fixed warp, hence I refer to it as a "short" warp. In this example, the loom is set at seven e.p.i., which I find is usually suitable for worsted, double knit, or sport yarn weights. Regardless of the width of the project, the warp is best placed centrally in the frame loom. This helps to keep the selvage tension even as you weave.

BEFORE YOU BEGIN

Mark the center point on the warp beam and cloth beam. Use this to measure and mark with tape the dents on which the warp will sit between both beams. These will be the first and last dents the warp is wound between to create the width needed for your project. Then, make sure all the wing nuts are tightly screwed.

Tools: Frame loom, warp yarn, and scissors.

1. Tie a loop with an overhand knot (see page 139) at the beginning of the warp yarn. Place the loop into the first two dents to the right of the taped mark. Feed the yarn down through the long heddle that corresponds with the first dent on the warp beam. (In this example, I start on the fourth dent and therefore the fourth long heddle on the heddle bar.)

2. Continue pulling the yarn under tension downward to the cloth beam. Feed the yarn through the fourth dent on the cloth beam. Catch the yarn around the cloth beam and feed upward through the fifth dent. Continue pulling the yarn upward under tension and feed it through the fifth long heddle on the heddle bar. (Make sure you skip the short heddles for now). Then feed the yarn upward through the fifth dent on the warp beam. This is where the loop is also threaded.

3. Continue winding the yarn up and down the frame loom, from warp beam to cloth beam and back. Ensure you thread the warp through the corresponding long heddle as you move across the frame from left to right. It's important to keep the tension the same across all warp threads, so keep the tension on the warp consistent as you wind. Repeat steps 1–3 until you have reached the last dent, marked by your tape. You have now wound half of the warp threads.

4. To wind the other half of the warp threads, you will dress the loom back in the opposite direction from right to left. This time, thread through the short heddles you skipped on the heddle bar. Thread over the same dents on the beams so that the threads are doubled.

5. The final warp thread will sit in a short heddle and finish back up at the warp beam **(5a)**. To finish, cut the yarn leaving a 2½ in. (6 cm) tail. While still maintaining the yarn tension, tie a loop with an overhand knot. Knot and place in the third and fourth dents **(5b)**.

6. Finally, make the heading cord (see page 32).

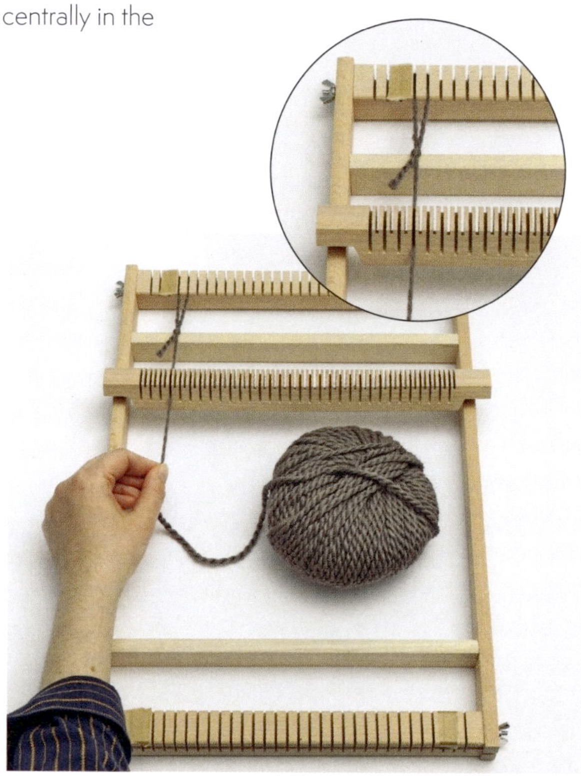

1

2

3

4

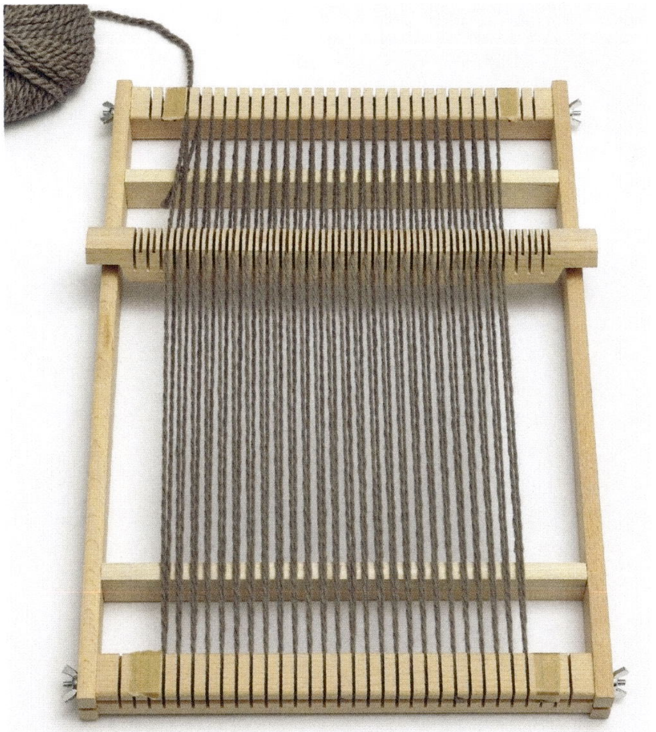

5a

5b

PREPARING A ROTATING (LONG) WARP

Dressing the loom with a rotating warp follows the same principle as for a fixed warp. The difference lies in the length of the warp. With a rotating warp, the beams are simply farther apart when warping, creating a longer warp. This is then wound up around the warp beam and fed on as needed, as you weave. It acts much the same way as a warp on a table or floor loom.

Tension is very important here. As you wind the warp around the warp beam, keep pulling it toward you, with a hand on either side of the beam. If you don't have a table the length of your warp, improvise by using the space between any two heavy, stationary pieces of furniture onto which you can clamp the loom.

TOOLS

Frame loom
A table or another solid surface the length of the warp (see above if this is not available)
Four clamps
Ten strips of cardboard cut to the size of the warp beam; the quantity needed depends on the length of the warp —in this example, the warp beam is 11 x 1 in. (28 x 2.5 cm)
Warp yarn
Scissors

Setting Up

1. Unscrew both wing nuts and detach the warp beam from the loom.

2. Using two clamps, secure the loom to the table edge on the cloth beam. Ensure the loom is straight, using the table edge as a guide. Measure the desired warp length—in this example my warp is 42 in. (110 cm). Using the remaining two clamps, secure the warp beam this distance from the cloth beam on the loom. The warp beam must align with the cloth beam, so that the dents line up and both beams are parallel. This is to ensure the warp threads are straight and under even tension.

Dressing the Loom

3. Dress the loom with a warp, following steps 1–5 of "Preparing a Fixed (Short) Warp" (see page 28).

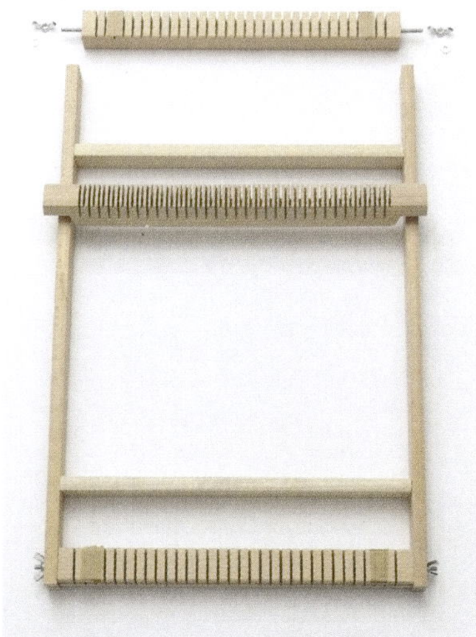

1

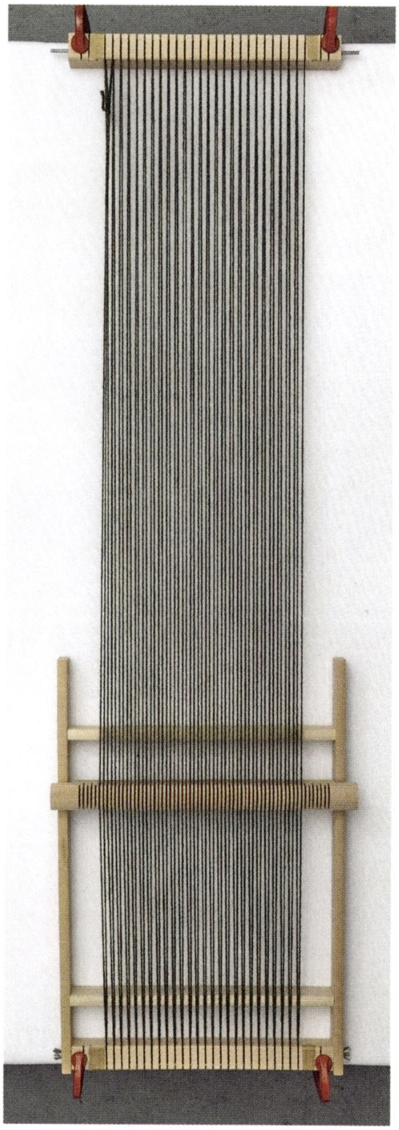

3

Winding the Warp

4. Once all the warp threads are measured and held under tension, carefully unclamp the warp beam from the edge of the table. With the clamps removed, keep the beam steady, retaining even tension across the width of the loom.

5. Place a cardboard strip over the open dents on the warp beam. Then, start winding by twisting the beam under and toward you. Holding the warp beam with both hands, continue to twist while keeping the warp even and under tension. When you have turned the beam on to all four sides, the cardboard strip will be visible again, now sandwiched between the beam and the warp.

6. Continue to wind, inserting a cardboard strip between the warp and beam after each turn, perpendicular to the warp. Each cardboard strip helps to prevent the warp threads sticking together and any threads slipping into the dents. Ensure each cardboard strip is straight and in line with the beam.

7. When the warp beam reaches the top of the frame loom, reattach it, securing with the wing nuts.

8. Next, make the heading cord (see following page).

4

5

6

7

MAKING THE HEADING CORD

The last step when dressing the loom with either a fixed or rotating warp is to make a heading cord. The heading cord acts as a firm horizontal base to weave upon and also helps to space the warp threads evenly. Heading cord yarn should be strong and tightly spun. It will be removed later but it is an important part of the process.

1. Tie a length of heading cord yarn tightly to the left-hand side of the frame loom, near the cloth beam where you wish to begin weaving. Tilt the heddle bar to create an opening (shed) through the warp threads. Pass the heading cord yarn through this shed.

1

2. Pull the heading cord yarn down toward the cloth beam. Pull firmly on the heading cord so that it is straight and perpendicular to the warp. Use your fingers or a fork (beater) to help straighten it by beating downward. Tie this end securely to the opposite side of the frame loom.

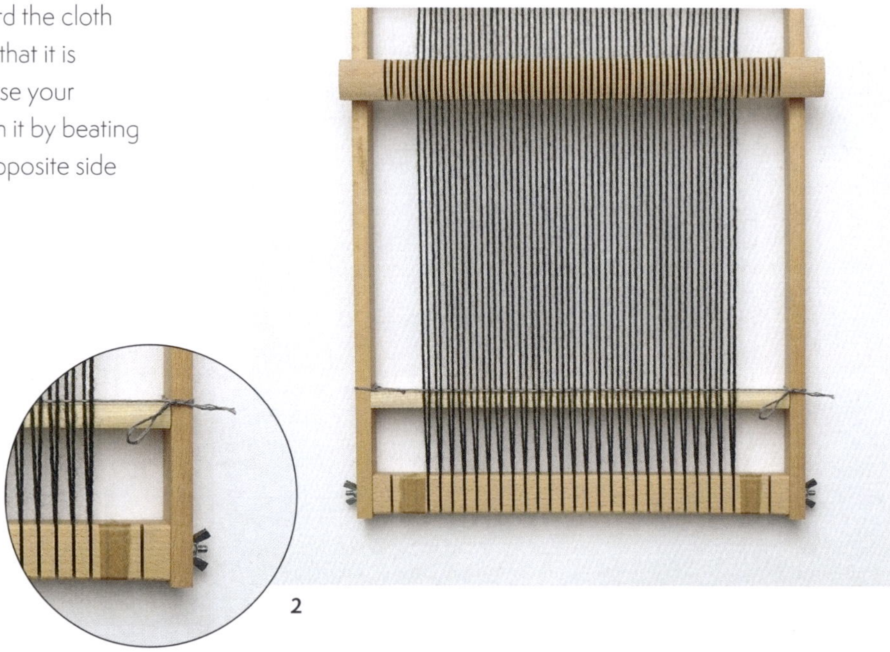

2

WINDING A STICK SHUTTLE

A stick shuttle is used to hold a length of weft yarn as you weave it through the warp threads.

1. Pointing the shuttle upward, place the tail end of the yarn through the indent. Wrap the yarn tightly around the shuttle a few times to hold the tail in place.

2. Bring the yarn through the indent once more, pull downward, and pass it through the indent at the other end of the shuttle. Bring the yarn back up and pass it through the first indent again. Wind the yarn from one indent to the other, wrapping it around the shuttle lengthwise until it builds up on both sides.

3. Stop winding when you have enough yarn and cut the yarn from the ball. Do not overfill the shuttle, as it needs to be slender enough to fit through the shed.

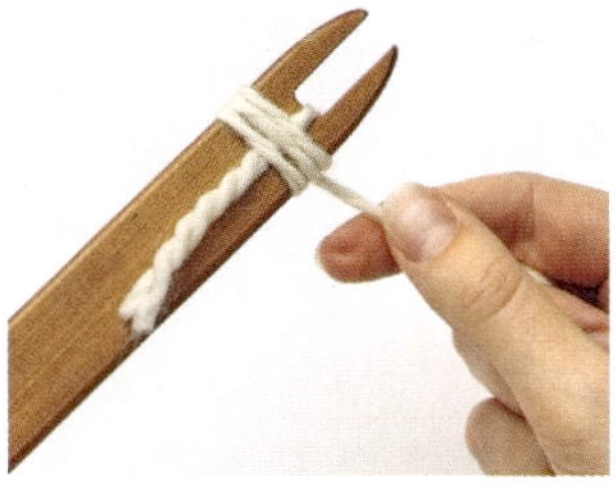

1

2

3

WINDING A FINGER SKEIN

A finger skein is often called a butterfly. You don't need any special tools—just your fingers and some yarn. A finger skein is very useful for shorter lengths of weft or for weaving multiple wefts. It is suitable for bulky wefts, as well as fine ones. You can easily change the size of a finger skein by widening or narrowing the space between your fingers.

1. Begin by passing the yarn between your thumb and index finger, leaving a tail to hang over the palm of your hand. Wrap the yarn around the outside of your thumb and pass it between your ring and little fingers. Wind the yarn in a figure eight around your little finger and thumb, as shown.

2. Fill up the skein by continuing to wind.

3. To tie off the yarn, bring the tail up over the top of the skein **(3a)** and then pull it down on the inside to form a loop **(3b)**.

4. Bring the tail of the yarn over the skein and pass it through the loop. Pull tight. Cut the yarn from the ball, about a hand's span from the skein. To remove the skein from your hand, pull upward. When you start weaving, you will feed the yarn with the long tail.

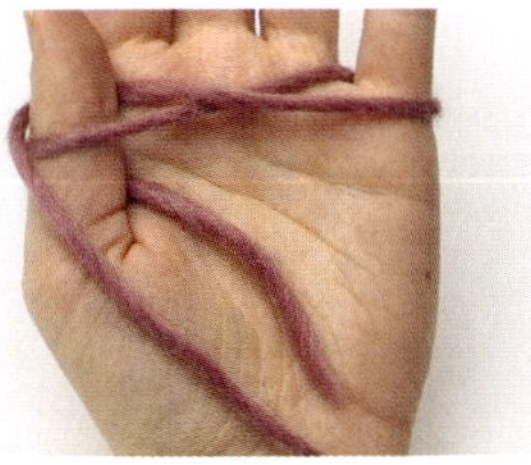

1

2

3a

3b

4

HANDWEAVING WITH A HEDDLE BAR

The heddle bar is a tool that can be used on any frame loom (for instructions on how to make your own, see page 134). Its purpose is to assist weaving in plain weave structure. The alternating slits (called "heddles") of long and short, on the heddle bar are used to create the two sheds of plain weave. By rocking the heddle bar back and forth, alternate warp threads are raised, which greatly speeds up weaving plain weave on a frame loom.

1. With the heddle bar threaded with the warp and positioned approximately three-quarters of the way up the warp as shown, twist the heddle bar upward and toward the warp beam. This allows the warp threads in the long heddles to be lowered, opening the first shed of plain weave. (The shed is the triangular space created for the weft to pass through.)

2. Pass the shuttle through the widest point of this shed, near the heddle bar. I usually begin weaving with my dominant hand (my right) weaving from right to left. Pass the shuttle through the shed from selvage (the closed woven edge on either side of the cloth) to selvage, right to left.

3. On this first pick (a single inserted row of weft yarn), hold onto the end of the weft yarn, keeping a tail of about 2½ in. (6 cm) on the right-hand side. Allow the weft to lengthen, by pulling the center of the weft upward with your finger to make an arc shape. This helps to prevent the selvages of your weaving from being drawn inward.

4. Tuck the weft tail around the outermost warp thread and weave it through the same shed, pulling the tail upward to sit on top of the weaving (after weaving a few rows you can trim the tail).

5. Close the shed to lock the weft in place by twisting the heddle bar back to its neutral position; all adjacent warp threads should rest flat at the same height. Using a fork, beat down the weft so that it lies straight and perpendicular to the warp threads. Begin by beating the center of the arc, then work out to each selvage.

6. With both hands, twist the heddle bar in the opposite direction, downward toward your weaving, as shown. This raises the warp threads in the long heddles, opening the opposite shed of plain weave. Pass the shuttle through the shed, this time in the opposite direction, from left to right. The shuttle will always be passed back from the same selvage that you just finished on the previous pick. As before, make an arc shape, twist the heddle bar to neutral, and beat. Repeat steps 1–6 to continue weaving.

1

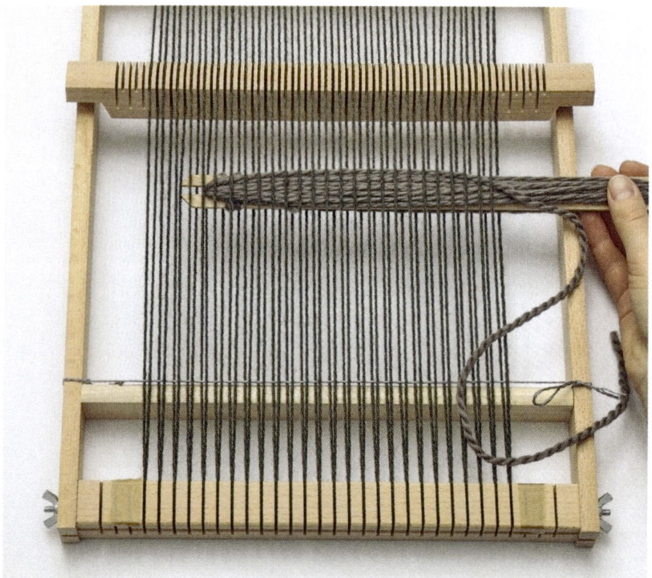

2

3

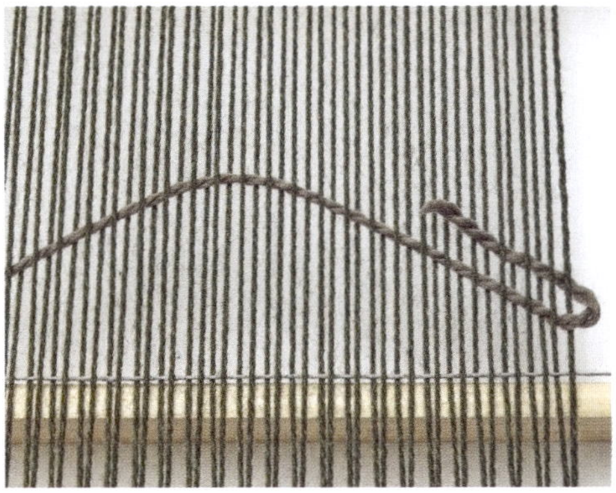

4

5

6

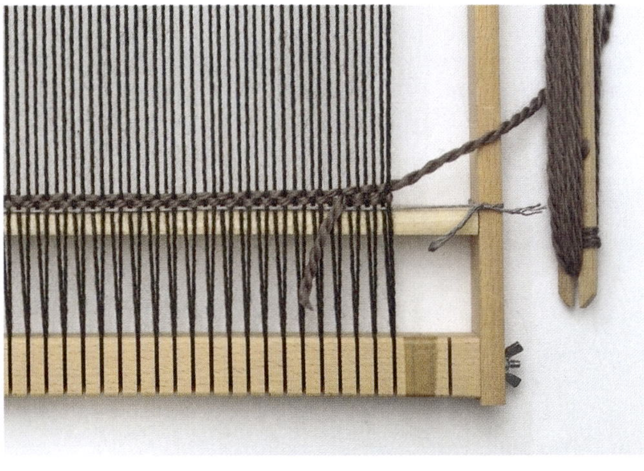

STICKY WARP THREADS?

If the warp threads are sticking together a little, insert your shed stick to help separate them. Pass the stick through the shed and pull it down to the fell of the cloth / weaving. Remove the stick before passing the weft through this shed.

PATTERNED WEAVING WITHOUT A HEDDLE BAR

Patterned weaving is achieved by changing the combinations of warp and weft interlacements and repeating these in sequences. Plain weave consists of alternating two sheds, where the weft travels over or under a warp thread on each alternate pick. So far, we have woven with plain weave. This section teaches you how to weave other weave structures without using a heddle bar.

A shed stick (or a pick-up stick) is used to weave a variety of structures (see the Weave Directory on pages 52–67). The shed stick allows you to individually select which warp threads you wish to lift, depending on the pattern or technique. Put simply, instead of using a heddle bar, you are using a shed stick to raise the warp threads and open the shed. But both heddle bar and shed stick can be used in combination. Furthermore, you can create a plain weave with a shed stick without a heddle bar. The heddle bar just makes it faster.

VERTICAL HERRINGBONE CHART

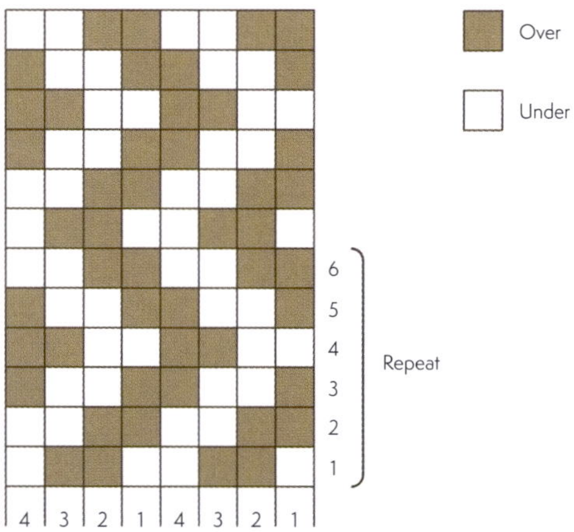

VERTICAL HERRINGBONE

The following instructions explain how to create a vertical herringbone weave structure, as shown in the chart.

BEFORE YOU BEGIN

In order to give yourself maximum weaving space when weaving with a shed stick, use the heddle bar and shed stick to wind the warp onto the loom.

1. Thread the shed stick through the warp threads following the chart, from right to left. The sequence repeats across four warp threads. The chart and key show that on the first pick (row 1), the weft must travel under the first warp thread, over the next two warp threads, and under the fourth warp thread. So, working from right to left, pass the stick through the warp threads as follows: under one warp thread; then over two warp threads, under two warp threads, and repeat until it reaches the opposite selvage.

2. When the shed stick has been threaded through the warp in the sequence indicated by the pattern, push the stick up toward the heddle bar. Twist the stick on its side to raise the warp threads and open the shed, as shown.

3. Follow steps 2–5 on page 34, using the shed stick in place of the heddle bar. When you have passed the shuttle through the shed, twist the shed stick flat and remove it before beating. The first row of the vertical herringbone pattern is complete.

4. For the second row of herringbone, thread the shed stick through the warp, following the chart. From right to left, the sequence is over two, under two, over two, under two, and so on, repeating the sequence across the warp to the opposite selvage. Pass the shuttle back through the shed, this time in the opposite direction, from left to right following the sequence. Once again, make an arc shape, twist the shed stick flat, and beat as before.

5. Repeat steps 1–4, progressing through the rows of the chart. This pattern repeats after six rows. Notice how the weft floats (where the weft lies over the warp threads) build up to form the striking herringbone chevrons.

1

2

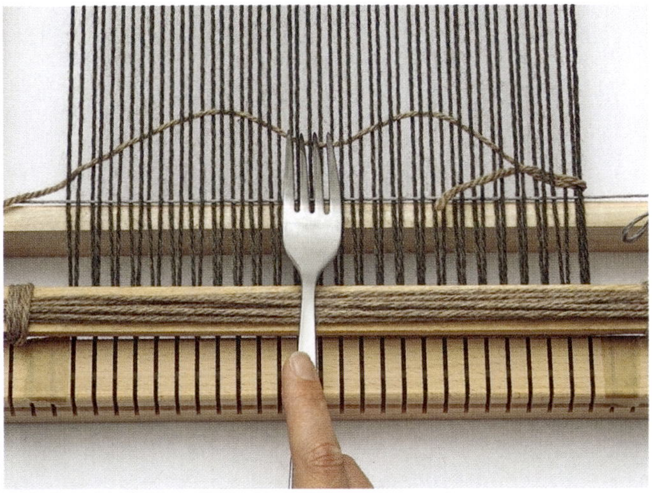

3

4

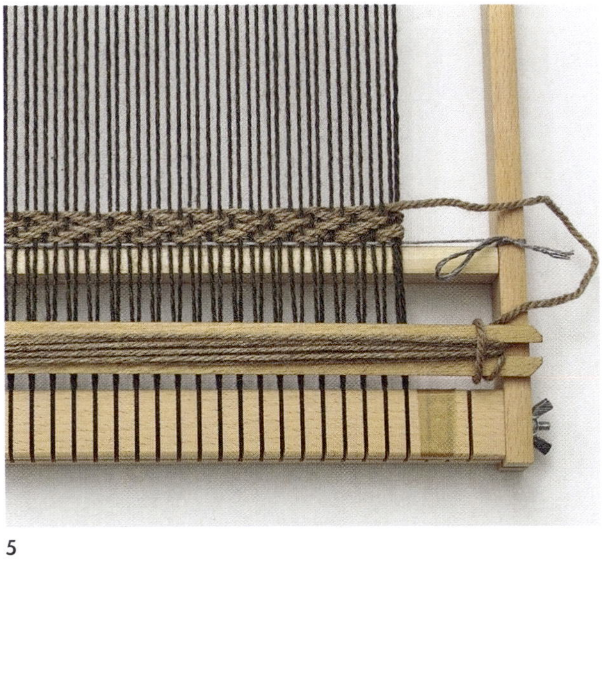

5

VERSATILE SHED STICK

This method is also used to weave any weave structure with a shed stick. The heddle bar is also detachable (slant the heddle bar and pull downward off the reverse of the warp), but I leave it in place on the warp. This way, I can easily weave up some plain weave on the same warp. It also helps to keep the warp threads evenly spaced. When using both the heddle bar and shed stick together, wind the warp on before weaving with the shed stick to give yourself maximum weaving space.

ADVANCING THE WARP

When weaving on a rotating warp, once the shed becomes too small to comfortably pass the weft through, it is time to advance the warp.

1. Lay the frame loom flat on a table. Note the tension of the warp, by lightly feeling with your hand. Loosen both wing nuts on the warp beam.

2. Twist the warp beam in the direction of the weaving, releasing the warp for two full rotations. The warp will become quite slack, so be careful not to let the warp threads jump out of the heddle bar.

3. The first time you advance the warp, you will need to remove the heading cord. Snip the heading cord at one side of the frame loom and gently pull it out of the warp threads from the opposite side.

4. Tighten the wing nuts on the warp beam, to stop the warp unwinding any further. Remove any of the cardboard strips as they fall out.

5. Loosen the two wing nuts on the cloth beam at the bottom of the frame loom and rotate it. Twist the beam away from the frame loom, toward you (this tightens the warp). Continue to tighten until the warp is of similar tension to before you began advancing the warp.

6. Tighten the wing nuts on the cloth beam and push the heddle bar back up to its position near the top of the frame loom. Aim to wind the warp on until the fell of the cloth is approximately 2½ in. (6 cm) above the cloth beam. This may take a few tweaks—repeat steps 1–5 until you are happy with the placement and tension of the warp.

WARP TENSION

To adjust the tension of the warp only, make sure that one set of wing nuts is tight to hold the warp in place. Loosen the other set of wing nuts. Twist the opposite beam away from the tightened beam, so that the warp thread pulls against it, making the warp taut. You can do this while you are weaving if you feel the tension has slackened. Twist in the opposite direction if the warp is too taut.

1

2

3

4

5

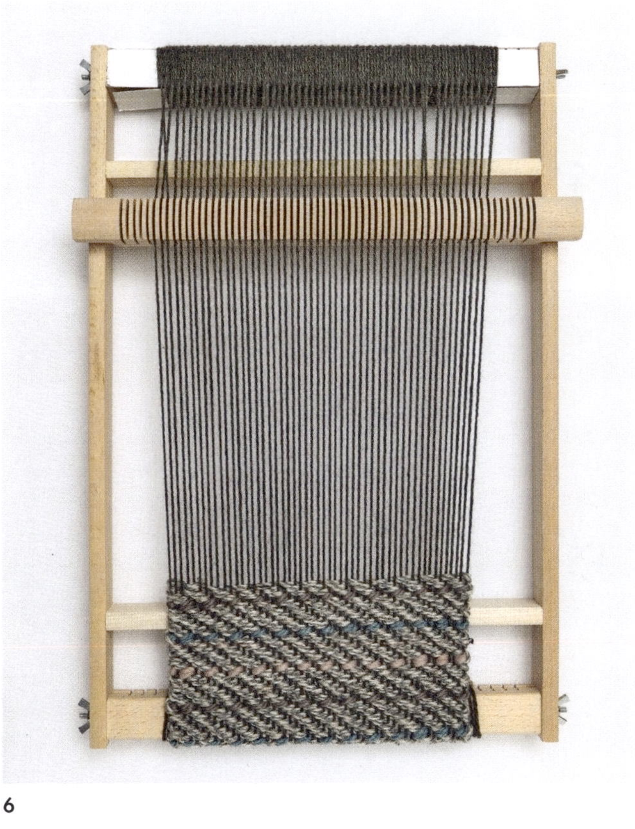

6

REMOVING YOUR WEAVING FROM THE LOOM

To avoid wasting leftover warp yarn, finish weaving as close to the heddle bar (or if you're not using a heddle bar, then as close to the top of the frame loom) as possible. As the fell of the cloth grows closer to this point, it becomes increasingly difficult to weave. The shed will become smaller and the tension can slip. I often use a long, flat needle such as a nålbinding needle to weave those final few picks.

Before you take your piece from the loom, it is worth considering how you would like to edge the cloth. As the warp threads are stretched in tension while on the loom, once cut they will relax and shorten a little. This means the last few picks can potentially slide out. The way to overcome this and prevent your weaving unraveling is to use an edging technique. If you are hemstitching your weaving, remember to do so before you take your piece off the loom. For hemstitching instructions and more edging techniques, see pages 48–51.

Releasing the Fabric from the Warp Beam

If working on a long warp, follow these three steps for the warp beam, then the three steps on the opposite page. If working on a fixed warp (a short warp—the length of the frame loom only), follow these three steps on the warp beam, then repeat them for the opposite end of the warp, on the cloth beam.

1. Loosen the wing nuts on the warp beam and twist the beam downward, toward the weaving. This slackens the warp and releases the warp loops.

2. Keep twisting the warp beam until all loops are released. With sharp scissors, carefully snip the warp loops in two at the top of each loop.

3. Remove the heddle bar by pulling upward, combing through the warp threads.

1

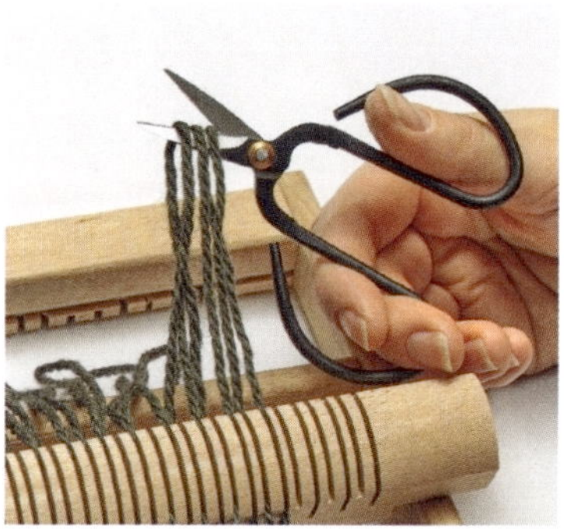

2

3

1

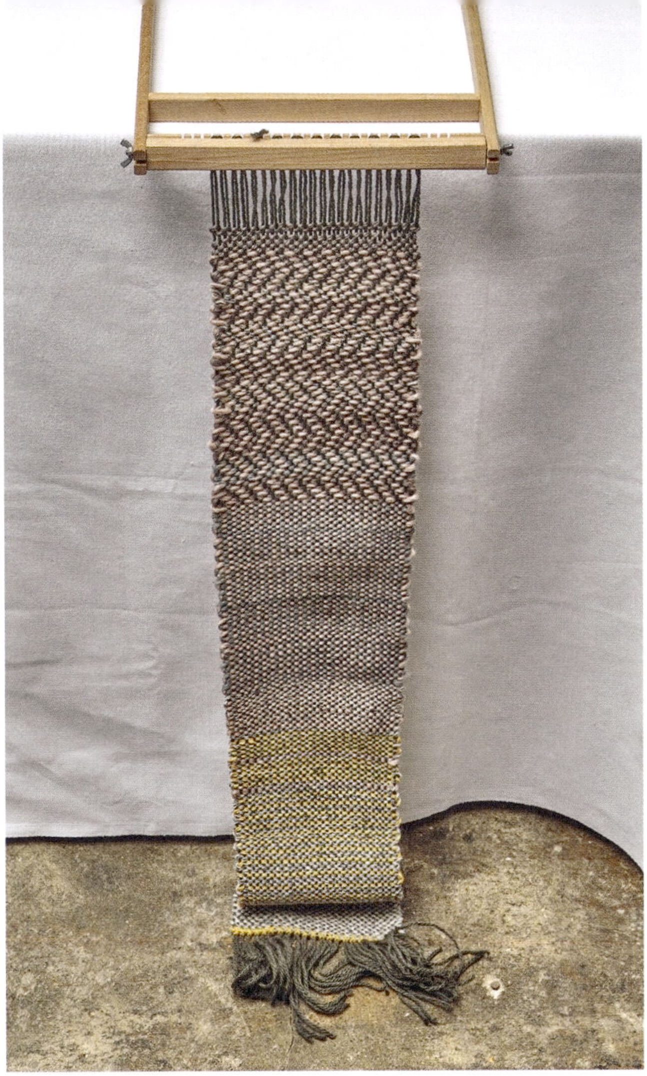

2

3

Unrolling the Cloth Beam (on a Long Warp)

When working on a long warp, this is always a very satisfying moment, whatever type of loom you are weaving on—be it a rigid heddle loom, table loom, floor loom, or frame loom! It's the moment of revisiting all your weaving thoughts as you created the piece. It's the first reveal of a long length of cloth, all woven by your hands. The longer the warp, the more exciting the reveal! After all the meticulous weaving, you will be relieved to know that this is a rather simple process.

1. Loosen both wing nuts on the cloth beam. Rest the warp beam over the edge of the table, with the end of the warp you just cut from the loom hanging downward, toward the floor.

2. Twist the cloth beam backward, toward the center of the frame loom. Let go of the cloth beam and let all the weaving unroll.

3. As you did on the warp beam at the other end of the loom, release any warp loops caught in the dents and snip with sharp scissors.

That's it—now you can enjoy the reward of admiring your very own weaving!

WOVEN TECHNIQUES

FLOATS AND TASSELS

The art of weaving has been in existence for millennia, and in this section I show you just three of the many techniques that have evolved in the hands of countless craftspeople. Each technique has its own origins, deriving from periods and places as far-reaching as Ancient Peru and Roman Egypt, to be later refashioned in eighteenth-century Britain, pre-nineteenth-century southeastern Europe, and beyond.

The floats and tassels (extra weft) technique adds a textured, decorative detail to any woven cloth, from furnishing to fashion fabrics. It can be dense and shaggy with a high pile, or simply an edging detail on a block of color.

FLOATS AND TASSELS: EXTRA WEFT

- This chart should be read from bottom to top, right to left. After the fourth row, the pattern repeats.
- Both shades of blue indicate the same continuous extra weft.

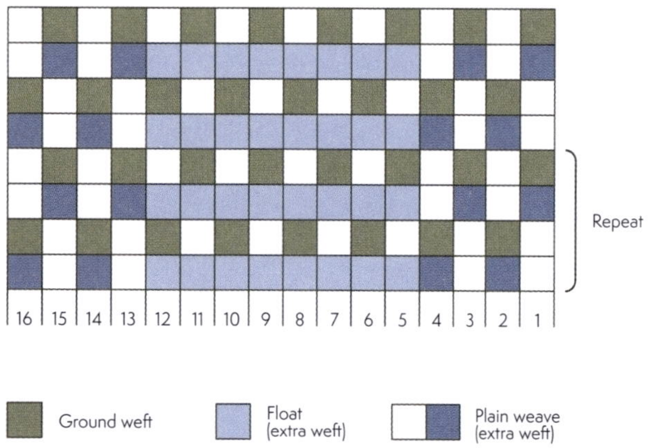

TOOLS

Frame loom
Beater (or fork)
Shed stick
Two shuttles
Ground-weft yarn (plain weave)
Extra-weft yarn (floats and tassels)
Scissors

BEFORE YOU BEGIN

To prepare, weave four rows of plain weave in ground-weft yarn, leaving this shuttle attached. The chart is worked over multiples of sixteen warp threads. In this example, the warp has forty-eight threads, but you could dress your loom to suit its size and your preference.

1. For the first extra-weft pick, use the shed stick to pick up the desired warp threads, as shown in the chart. The shed stick will pass under one, over one, under one, over nine, under one, over one, under one, over one. Repeat this sequence across to the warp. Pass the extra-weft shuttle through the created shed. Leave this shuttle attached.

2. After beating, weave the next row with the ground weft in plain weave, using the heddle bar, as per the chart. Leave this shuttle attached.

3. Weave the next row using the extra-weft yarn. Using the shed stick, raise the warp threads for the second extra-weft pick. Note that on this pick, you are picking up the opposite plain weave shed in the woven blocks. The floats sit over the same blocks of warp threads, like the first pick.

4. After beating the extra-weft row, raise the opposite shed of plain weave as per the chart. Weave with the ground weft yarn.

Repeat these four picks of the chart (steps 1–4) until you have the length of cloth you desire. In this example, I have woven eight picks of extra weft (four repeats of steps 1–4, following the chart).

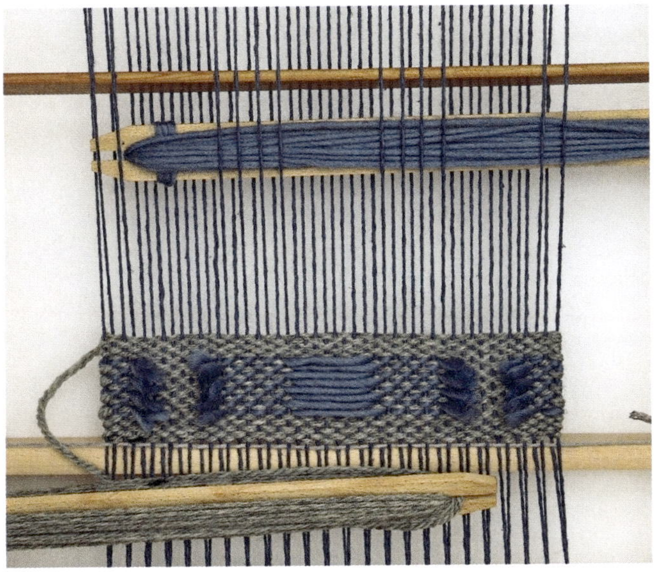

1

2

3

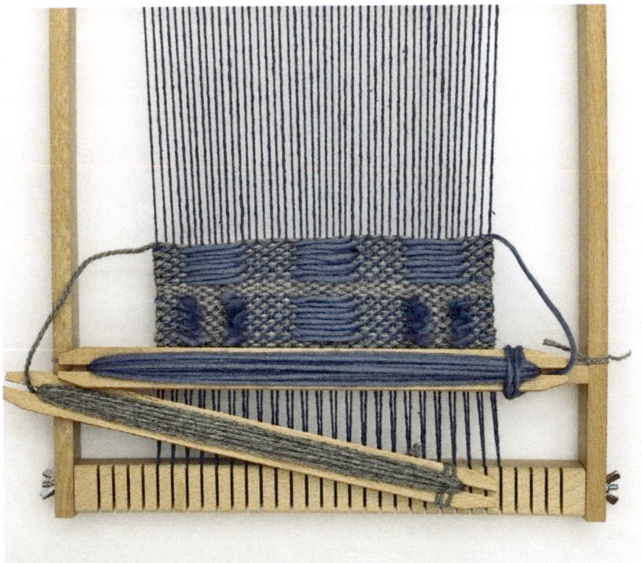

4

5. To transform the floats into tassels, cut the floats with sharp scissors. For the trimmed tassels in this example, make two cuts in the floats as follows: from the right-hand side of the float block, count in three warp threads and make the first vertical cut here, ensuring you cut all weft floats. Repeat this from the left-hand side of the float block, using the warp threads as a guide.

Measure in three warp threads and make the second vertical cut here. Remove any excess yarn. (For zero waste, the excess trimmings can be collected to use as stuffing or for a felting project.)

You can also choose to leave blocks of floats uncut for a varied extra-weft texture. Try creating a combination of trimmed tassels and float blocks for added interest.

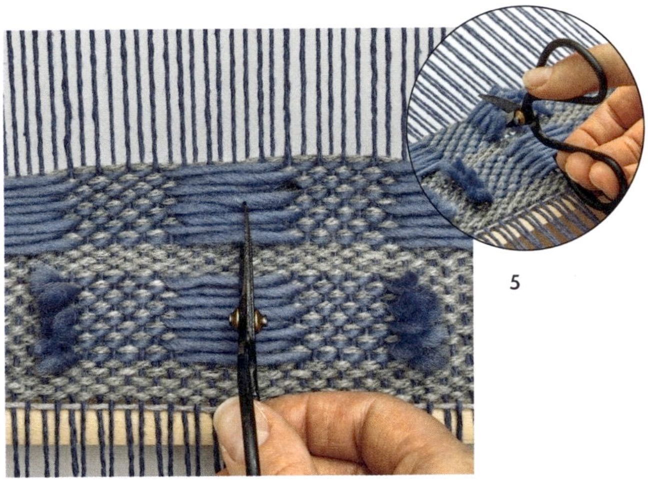

5

VERTICAL SOUMAK

This is a raised surface decoration technique, used in traditional rug making. It is made with a supplementary weft and can be used in plain and patterned weaving.

In this variation of soumak, the weft is wrapped around the warp threads vertically, as opposed to horizontally in its more common form. It results in vertical stripes and an intriguing knit-like texture, with echoes of a purl stitch. I like this variation of soumak, as the warp and ground weft remain visible, with the opportunity for more color to subtly seep into the piece. As a bonus, it is also structurally sound!

TOOLS

Frame loom
Beater (or fork)
Finger skeins of extra-weft yarn (this works best if the weft yarn is thicker than the warp yarn)
Ground-weft yarn (plain weave)

1

1. Wind finger skeins of the extra-weft yarn twice the length of the warp ends you wish to cover. Wind one finger skein for every two warp ends. Attach each finger skein to the warp ends with a lark's head knot (see page 139) as follows: beginning on the right-hand side, working in blocks of four warp ends, tie a lark's head knot on the first two warp ends with the loop facing inward (to the left). Tighten and pull the knot downward to sit next to the previous weft pick. Pull the short tail to the back.

2. On the next two warp ends (the third and fourth), tie a lark's head knot with the loop facing the opposite way, outward (to the right). Tighten so that the knots mirror each other.

3. Repeat for the pairs of knots across the row or enough to cover all the warp threads you wish.

4. After weaving four rows of plain weave of ground weft, take the first finger skein on the right and pass it behind the first two warp threads, from right to left. Pull the finger skein up to the front of the weaving, between the second and third warp ends. Pull tight.

5. Pass the second finger skein under the next two warp ends (the third and fourth) in the opposite direction, from left to right. Pull the finger skein up to the front of the weaving, between the second and third warp end. Pull tight.

6. Working in pairs of finger skeins on blocks of four warp ends, repeat across the row.

7. Repeat steps 4–6 until you achieve the desired length of vertical soumak.

8. To finish, pass the first finger skein under the first two warp ends as in step 4. Pass the weft over the second warp end and under, as shown **(8a)**. Tighten the first loop.

To secure, bring the weft to the front, between the second and third warp ends. Pass the weft under the loop just created, as shown. Tighten and pull the weft to the reverse. Repeat for the second finger skein over the third and fourth warp ends, working in the opposite direction, to create a mirror image **(8b)**. Repeat across the row for all weft pairs.

1 and 2

3

4

5

6

7

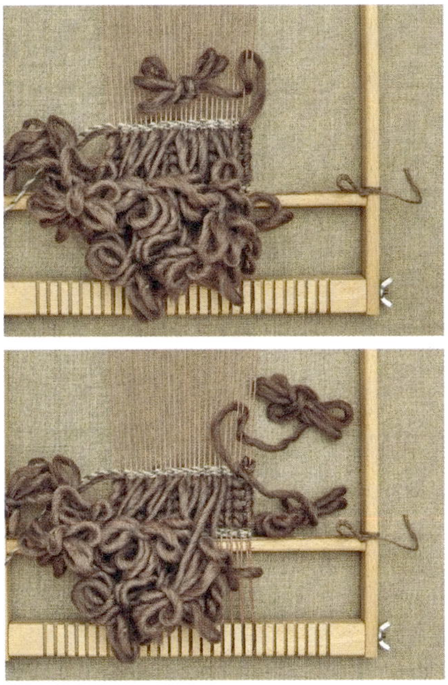

8a and 8b

LENO WEAVE

Leno weave is a fascinating hand process, during which the weaver manipulates the warp to create a lace weave. The gauze or mesh-like effect involves individually manipulating warp threads on the loom and holding them in place with a weft. The result is a warp-faced cloth that has a lot of stretch and movement.

Despite being an open-work cloth, the placement of weft within the twisted warp threads gives it great stability. However, there is shrinkage with this structure that must be considered when planning your project. It can shrink as much as 50 percent of the warp width. An idea to help maintain the warp width is to make a "temple" using a paper clip and elastic tied to the edge of the frame loom, as shown in this example. This leno is called a "2/2 Leno" and is worked in blocks of four warp threads, twisting the pairs of warp threads around each other. It is most effective when the same yarn is used for both warp and weft.

TOOLS

Frame loom
Beater (or fork)
Shed stick
Shuttle
Two temples (elastic and paperclip)

Using a Temple

A temple is a device used to stretch the woven warp, helping maintain its width and preventing too much shrinkage. By tying the elastic close to the side bar of the loom, the weaving is stretched outward when hooked with the paper clip. Unhook and move the temples as you weave.

LENO WEAVE

This chart should be read from bottom to top, right to left.
After the eighth row, the pattern repeats.

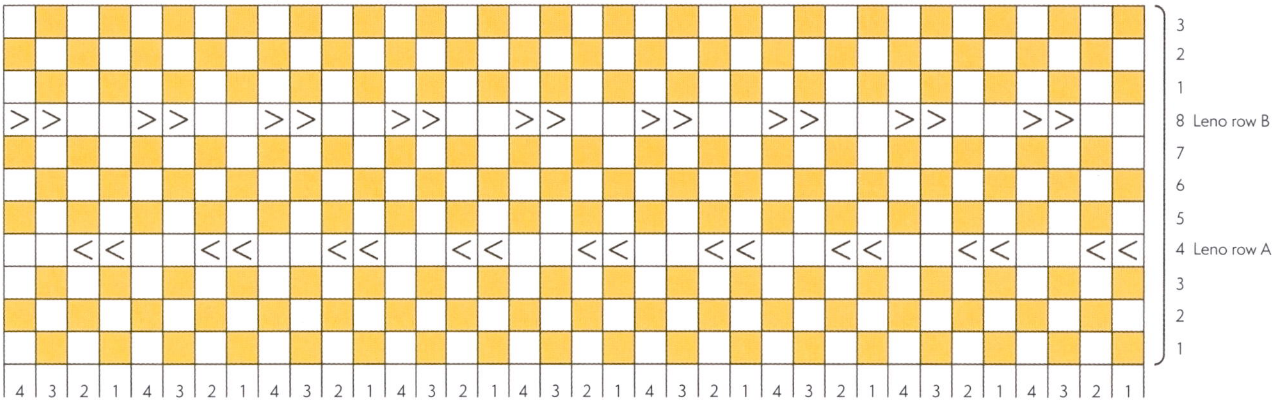

Over
Under
Pass over to the left
Pass over to the right

1

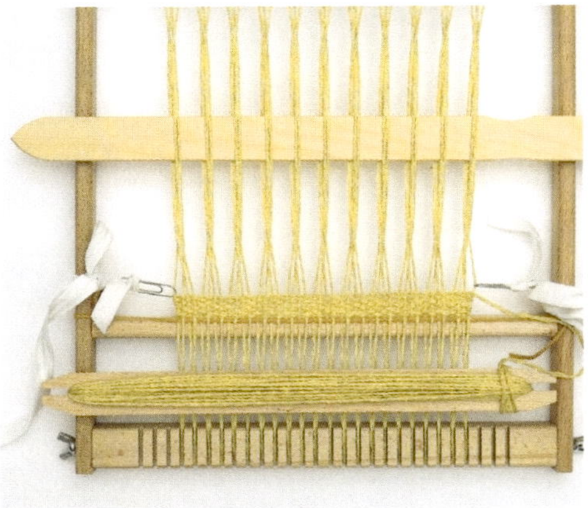

2

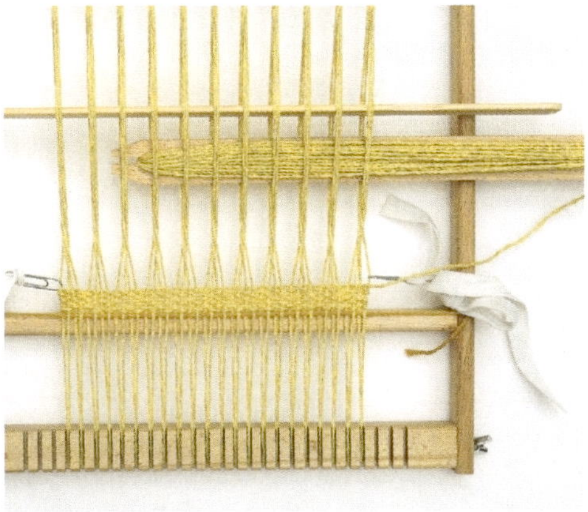

3

In this example, the warp has forty-eight threads, but you could dress your loom to suit its size and your preference.

1. To prepare, weave four rows of plain weave in ground-weft yarn, leaving this shuttle attached. Weave three rows of plain weave following the chart. Then on the fourth row, labeled on the chart as "Leno row A," working right to left, select the first two warp threads and cross them over the third and fourth warp threads toward to the left. Use the shed stick to hold the twist by inserting it in between the two pairs of warp threads as follows—under the third and fourth warp thread (now on the right-hand side), then over the first and second warp threads (now on the left-hand side).

2. Continue twisting the pairs of warp threads across the warp by repeating step 1 until the stick is completely threaded through the warp.

3. Twist the shed stick on its side to open the leno shed. Pass the shuttle through this shed. For the best placement of the leno weft, place the stick close to the fell of the weaving, creating a short shed.

4. Beat the weft gently, leaving a gap between the previous pick and the leno pick. As you beat, ensure this pick is even and straight, being careful not to let the edges draw in too much.

5. Remove the shed stick and weave the next pick of plain weave, as per the chart. If the warp ends are twisting, use the stick to help separate them into the shed. Beat gently to straighten the weft, leaving an equal height gap between the leno pick and the previous block of plain weave.

6. After weaving the next two picks of plain weave, you are ready for the next leno pick, labeled on the chart as "Leno row B." Work in the same blocks of four warp threads, this time twisting the pairs of warp threads around each other in the opposite direction as follows—select the third and fourth warp thread and pass over the first and second warp threads toward the right. Insert the shed stick to hold the twist. This time the stick passes over the third and fourth warp threads (now on the right-hand side) and under the first and second warp threads (now on the left-hand side).

7. Continue across the row, repeating step 6 until all pairs of warp threads are twisted. Weave the next three rows of plain weave as per the chart, following step 5 for the first of these rows.

Repeat steps 1–7 until you achieve the desired length of leno weave.

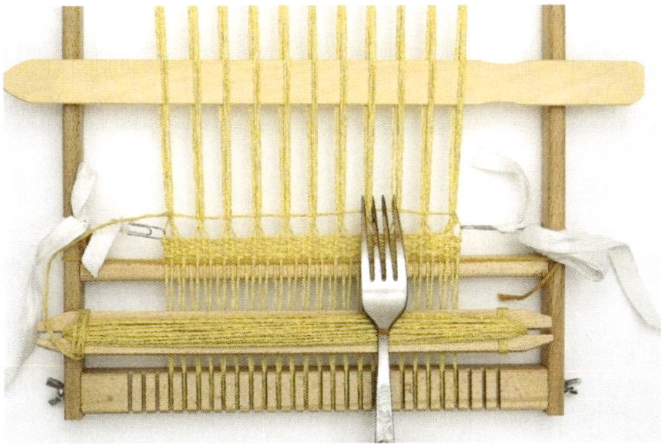

4

5

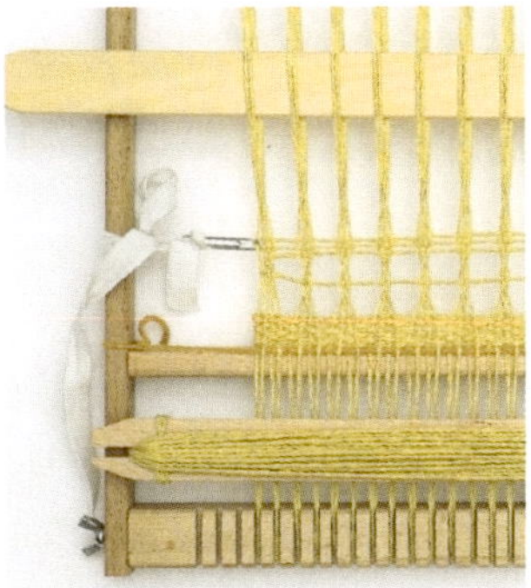

6

7

EDGING TECHNIQUES

HEMSTITCHING

Hemstitching is my favorite edging technique for frame-loom weaving. It can be sewn in the same yarn as the weft yarn to leave a nearly invisible finish. It is sewn when the piece of weaving it still in tension on the loom.

1. Thread a darning needle with sufficient yarn (you'll need about three times the length of the warp width). Beginning on the reverse side of the weaving, sew a double stitch into the selvage to secure the end. Working from the front side of the weaving, pass the needle under the first two warp ends at the right-hand selvage, moving from right to left. Pull the needle through completely with the yarn following.

2. Pass the thread back over these two warp threads, from left to right. Bring the needle from the reverse side through to the front, surfacing beyond the two warp threads that you just wrapped. Stitch in, two weft shots deep. Try to also catch a warp thread with your needle, to make the stitch more secure. Pull the yarn tight so that the warp threads are pulled together to form a fringe.

3. Repeat steps 1–2 to create more fringes until you reach the left-hand selvage.

4. To secure at the left-hand selvage, sew another double stitch on the reverse side of the weaving, as before. To tuck the tail, thread the needle through a few stitches on the reverse. Trim the yarn here.

5. After cutting and pulling out the heading cord, repeat the process across the bottom, or beginning, of the piece of weaving. When you have finished hemstitching both ends, cut the warp threads as far away from the weaving as possible. Then trim the fringe to the desired length.

1

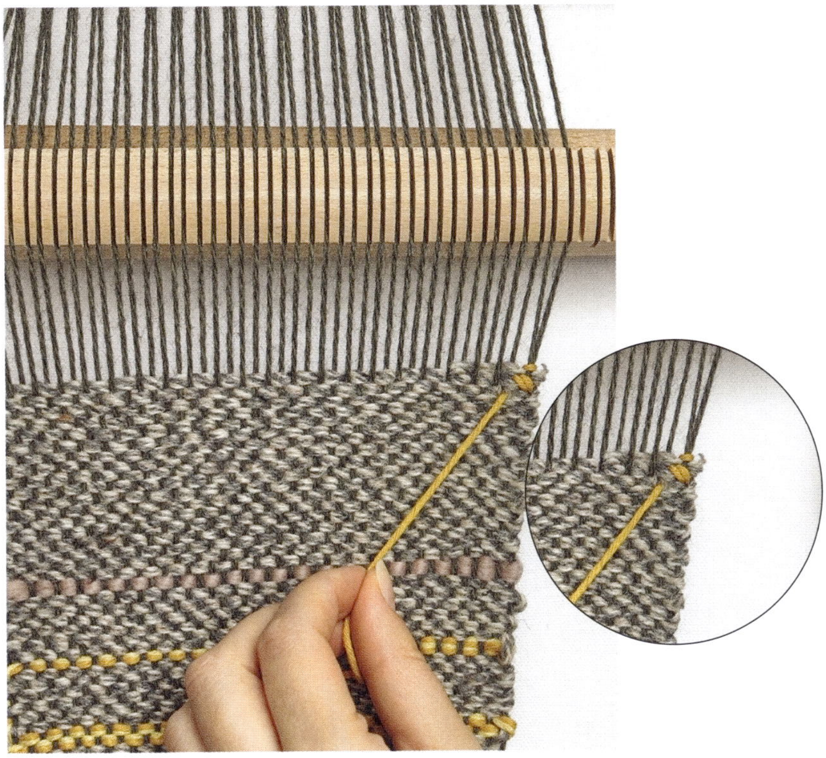

2

3

4

FRINGING

Fringing is an edging technique that occurs when you cut the weaving off of the frame loom. The number of ends you choose to group together for your fringe depends on the sett, yarn thickness, and personal preference.

1. Using scissors, cut the warp ends at the bottom of the frame loom, as close to the bottom bar as possible. Only cut about a quarter of the ends. Tie a group of warp ends together using an overhand knot (see page 139). To do this, make a loop close to the edge of the weaving and pull the ends through the loop. Here, I grouped four threads together. With a thicker yarn, you can group fewer threads together.

1

2. Tighten so that the knot sits close to the fell of the weaving. Continue cutting and tying off the ends in groups until you reach the other selvage. Once all the knots have been tied, trim the fringing to the desired length with a straight cut.

2

KNOT AND DARN EDGING

This edging technique is quite clean and flat. It does not lose any length in the woven piece and does not add any additional bulk. This technique is applied once the weaving has been removed from the loom.

1. After cutting the warp threads to leave a long fringe, take the weaving off of the loom and lay the piece flat, with the reverse side facing up. Beginning at the right-hand selvage, take the first two warp threads. Wrap the right-hand warp thread over and underneath the left-hand warp end, bringing the first thread back up through the loop it just formed. Pull upward, toward the weaving, to tighten. Taking the third warp end, repeat the same technique with the second warp end.

1

2. Continue working in this way, from right to left, across the entire warp. Thread the first warp end through a darning needle. For an invisible finish, darn the needle down through the weaving, following the pattern and path of that particular warp thread for about 1 in. (2.5 cm). Pull the needle all the way through. Continue threading the needle and darning each warp end in the same way.

Keep darning across the warp until you reach the other side of the piece. When all the warp ends have been darned, trim the tails close to the weaving.

2

WEAVE DIRECTORY

As explained earlier, the weaving process involves two sets of threads—vertical and horizontal—that interlace with each other. The sequence of interlacements is what defines a weave structure. This section introduces classic weave structures you may already be familiar with and even find in your closet or around your home. Houndstooth and herringbone are often used in classic tweed fashion fabrics. I associate the textured waffle weave more with crisp household textiles, while the pinwheel weave adds a playful, if dizzying, touch!

Each weave structure is illustrated with a chart and woven swatches. You'll need your shed stick at the ready (see page 36). We also delve a little deeper into the humble, simplest of structures—the plain weave—with four different plain weave variations. This section is intended as a reference guide for you to dip in and out of. It is also my hope to inspire you to create your own designs through experimenting. There really is so much value in sampling—this truly is where the magic can happen on the loom! This directory also provides insight into the "ingredients" of the project patterns in chapter three (see page 68).

VERTICAL HOUNDSTOOTH

Houndstooth is a classic tweed weave structure. Thought to originate in Scotland, the earliest examples were seen in woolen tweed cloth worn by shepherds in the Scottish Lowlands in the 1800s. Christian Dior's 1948 collection made it popular in the fashion world, and it has remained so through many reinventions.

It has a distinctive broken check-like form and, rather than squares, it consists of a specific repeating block. The name derives from the jagged tooth edge protruding from this block. Despite its intricate design, it is quite simple to weave, and is most often woven as a twill. In this example, it is woven as a 2/2 balanced twill, the simplest weave structure after plain weave. However, it is the placement of the color which transforms this weave from a twill to a houndstooth. The warp is striped in blocks of four warp threads, while the weft yarn alternates on each repeat of twill (four picks) to build up the houndstooth. For the most striking results, use highly contrasting colored yarns (light and dark) of the same weight. The trick is to also ensure the weave is completely balanced, with e.p.i. (ends per inch) and p.p.i. (picks per inch) in equal ratio. After repeating the sequence a few times, the pattern will emerge. Why not try mixing a few more colors into the houndstooth, perhaps creating a check?

WEAVE CHART

This chart should be read from bottom to top, right to left. After the eighth row, the pattern repeats.

Yarn A (dark)

Yarn B (light)

Under

VERTICAL HERRINGBONE

Herringbone weave, with its striking zigzag pattern, is a traditional weave structure often found in menswear fashion fabrics and tweeds. The name is evocative of the bare skeleton of the herring fish, the pattern echoing the diagonal bones that run the length of the herring's body.

First seen on brick roadways of Ancient Rome, the design was later introduced to textiles of the age. In more recent history, herringbone is seen as one of the classic tweed patterns often associated with Scotland and Ireland.
It is also synonymous with the high-end tailors of the iconic Savile Row in London. In this variation of the weave structure, the chevrons zigzag vertically, as opposed to the more commonly seen horizontal chevrons. It consists of rows of slanted diagonal lines, which shift direction after three picks, creating the chevron shape. This draft is worked over four warp threads and six picks. The first four picks consist of a 2/2 twill. After this, the pattern mirrors back for two picks, creating the distinctive chevron.

WEAVE CHART

This chart should be read from bottom to top, right to left. After the sixth row, the pattern repeats.

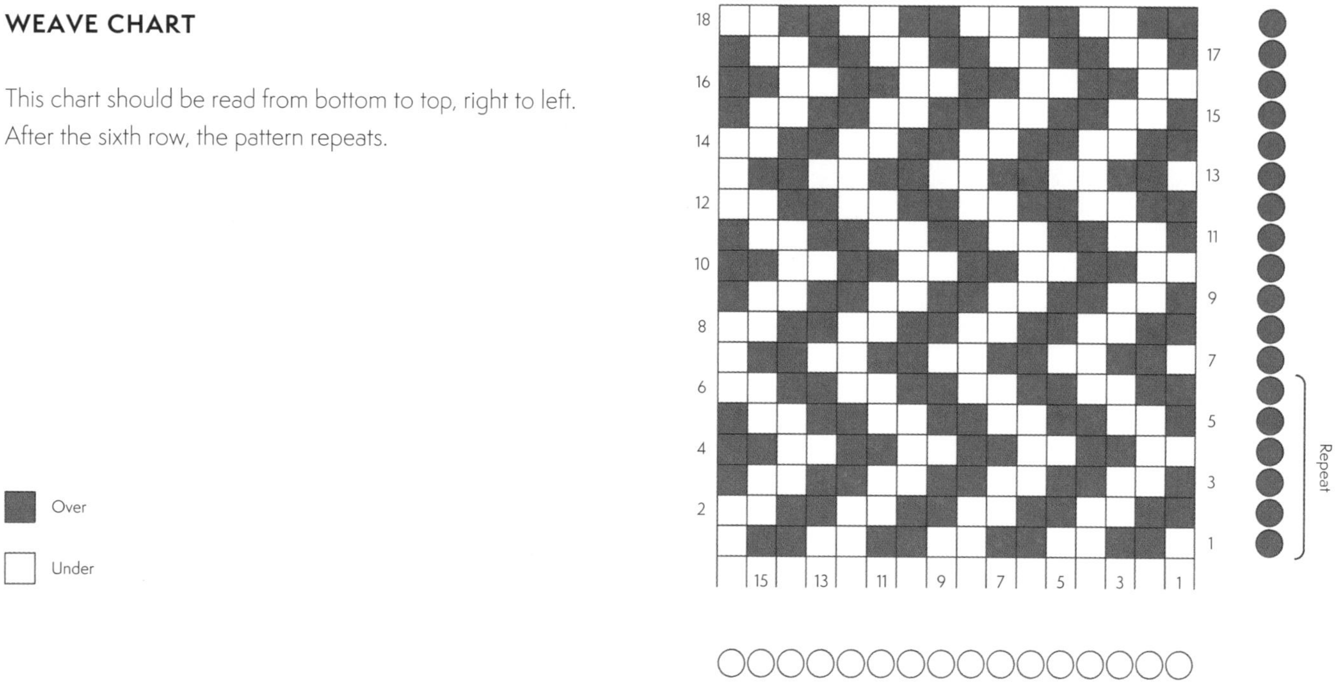

WAFFLE WEAVE

Waffle weave is such a fun, intriguing texture. The finished cloth resembles the squares of its sweet namesake. Its amazing, deep texture consists of cells framed by long warp and weft floats with a plain weave center.

This simple version of waffle weave is worked over six warp threads. Increasing the number of warp threads that the waffle is worked over will create a deeper waffle. Because of its structure, there are fewer warp and weft intersections. This means it draws in quite a bit and has a high level of shrinkage (at least 30 percent shrinkage, before even considering the fiber). So it is a good idea to plan for this when designing your waffle weave project. This weave works best on a tightly set warp. I often set the warp one-third tighter than normal for the yarn weight, such as 12 e.p.i. instead of 8 e.p.i. Remember to beat tightly.

When on the loom the waffles are almost flat, but they really come alive once out of tension, off the loom, and gently hand washed. I love experimenting with color in this structure—using the same color for the long warp and weft floats is key to creating a really defined cell. Using a color gradient of yarn to echo the depth of the cell could also have very interesting results.

WEAVE CHART

This chart should be read from bottom to top, right to left. After the sixth row, the pattern repeats.

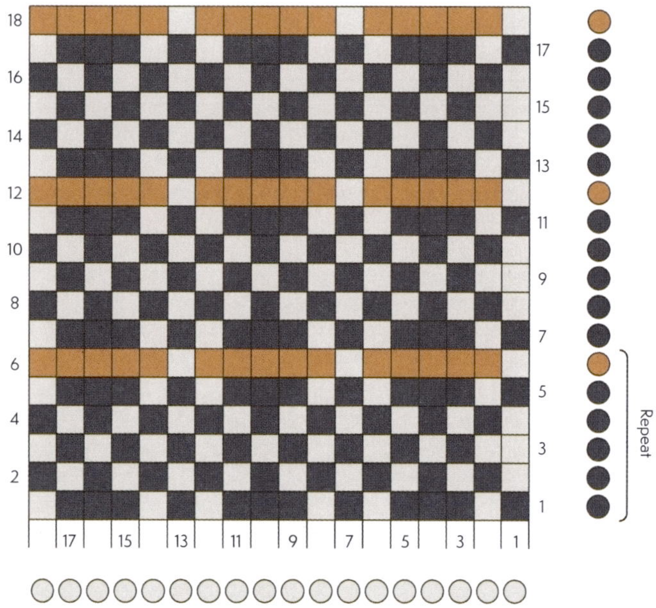

Over

Under

Same color as warp yarn

PINWHEEL

Pinwheel is a fun, playful weave structure featuring dynamic swirls of color. It is reminiscent of childhood toys and lawn ornaments with sails that twirl in the breeze. In Chinese culture, the pinwheel is used to represent good fortune and carries with it the wish to "turn one's luck around."

The earliest examples of the pinwheel design in textiles is thought to have been seen in embroidered quilts of nineteenth-century American textiles, with the pinwheel representing the common sight of windmills in small farming towns across the country in the nineteenth and early-twentieth centuries. It is possible that the design was introduced to woven textiles—quilts and coverlets—also around this time. The woven pinwheel design is constructed with a striped warp. The weft alternates light and dark color blocks and consists of a series of incremental floats combined with a plain weave center. The pattern emerges after being repeated at least three times. As with other weave structures, it works best with yarns of equal weight and spacing.

WEAVE CHART

This chart should be read from bottom to top, right to left. After the sixteenth row, the pattern repeats.

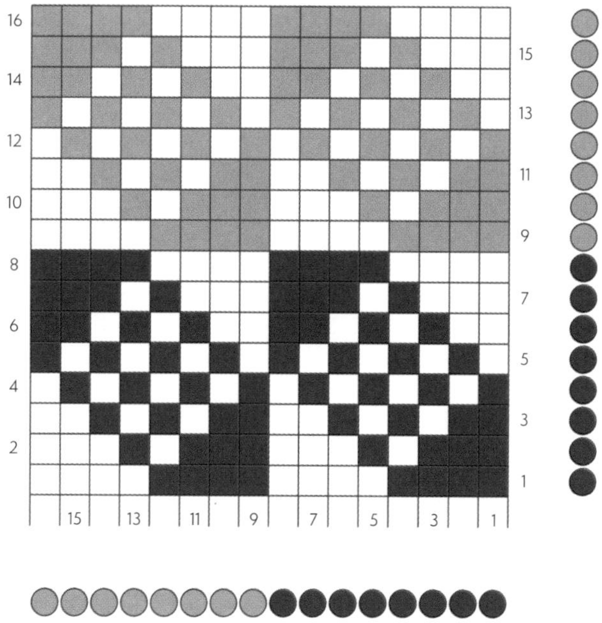

Yarn A (dark)

Yarn B (light)

Under

PLAIN WEAVE VARIATIONS

This section introduces the potential of plain weave. Through the creative use of "color and weave effects," plain weave can take on very different forms while still being woven under one, over one, under one, over one, and so on. This is achieved through the clever placement of color, tricking the eye. I love using these techniques, as they truly are optical illusions with weave! The structure always remains the noble plain weave, but it is the change of color sequence which gives it a complex appearance. Using plain weave variations in combination with each other is the basis of one form of weave design known as "color patterns." As this book focuses on using a frame loom with a heddle bar (easing the weaving of plain weave), I hope this section inspires you to explore what the simplest of weave structures has to offer, in this selection of variations—of which there are many, many more!

LOG CABIN

Log cabin beautifully demonstrates the potential of "color and weave effects," being simple to weave yet mesmerizing to look at. The first time I saw log cabin, I could not quite get my head around how it could possibly be woven as a single cloth, instead giving the impression that layers of cloth are woven in and out of each other.

Log cabin consists of blocks alternating between vertical and horizontal stripes. Two colors of equal yarn weight are needed, and it works best with highly contrasting tones, such as light and dark. The basic principle of this pattern is that the two colors alternate for a block, then the alternating shifts to create the next block. In this example, the colors alternate between white (A) and gray (B) four times, then B is repeated so that two B threads sit side by side. Then the alternating continues for the next block, as shown in the chart opposite. Experiment by introducing a third color. Try contrasting different textures of yarns for an alluring effect, and remember—the blocks do not always need to be the same size.

WEAVE CHART

This chart should be read from bottom to top, right to left.
After the sixteenth row, the pattern repeats.

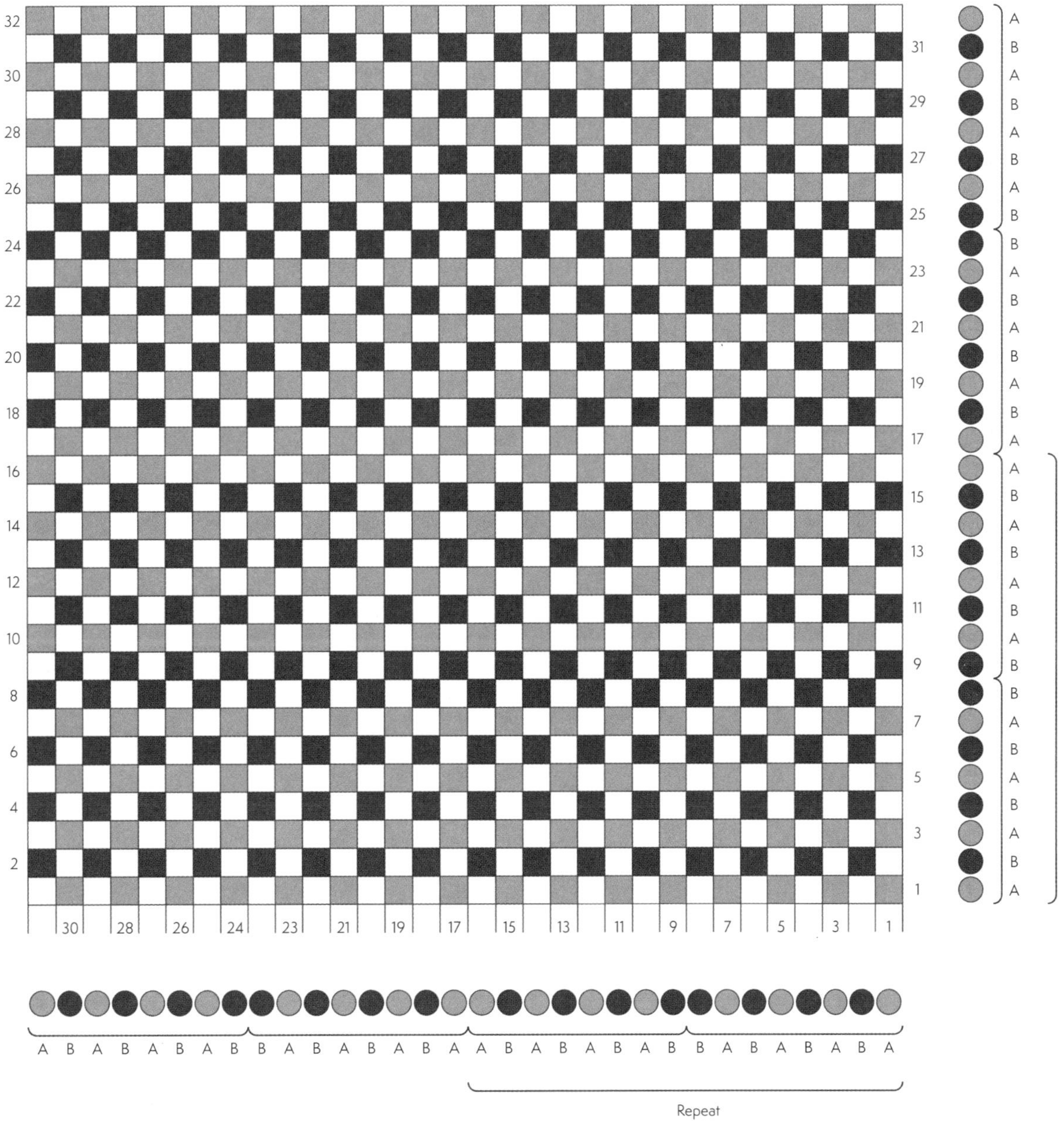

Yarn A (light)

Yarn B (dark)

Under

PLAIN HOUNDSTOOTH

I love this version of houndstooth, as it feels like a sneaky cheat! The wonderfully jagged tooth edges can also be created through the interlacement of plain weave sheds, together with color. For the most striking houndstooth, weave with two colors—a light yarn and a dark yarn of equal weight.

The construction involves repeating the same warp sequence across the weft. For example, two white warp ends, two purple warp ends (repeat), woven with two white picks, two purple picks (repeat). As with other plain weave variations, it needs to be a balanced weave (with the e.p.i. and p.p.i. in equal ratio) for the best effect. To liven up this houndstooth, you can add more colors, but keep tone in mind since this pattern works best with a strong dark and light contrast. In this sample, I have used four colors, keeping white as the light yarn, while a dark purple, light purple, and yellow act as the darker yarns to create contrast.

WEAVE CHART

This chart should be read from bottom to top, right to left. After the fourth row, the pattern repeats.

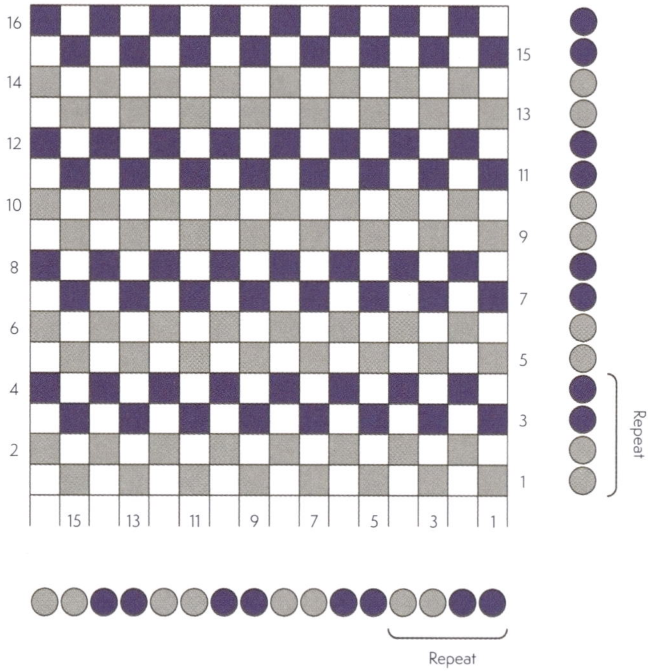

Yarn A

Yarn B

Under

1/1 COLOR

This is a plain weave variation that I love incorporating into my designs. It's a very subtle way of adding extra depth and color to a pattern. The name comes from the order of colors in the warp—alternating one end of the first color (A), with one end of the second color (B), throughout the warp.

This warp is full of so many possibilities, depending on how it is woven. I have no doubt you'll have fun experimenting with this one—here are a few ideas to get you started:

- Weave the weft solidly with one of these two colors to create dots.
- Bring in a third color (C) to alternate throughout the weft, adding further depth.
- Alternate the weft with one pick of yarn A and one pick of yarn B to create vertical stripes on one side of the weave, with horizontal stripes on the reverse side (as seen in the infinity scarf, page 78).

WEAVE CHART

This chart should be read from bottom to top, right to left.

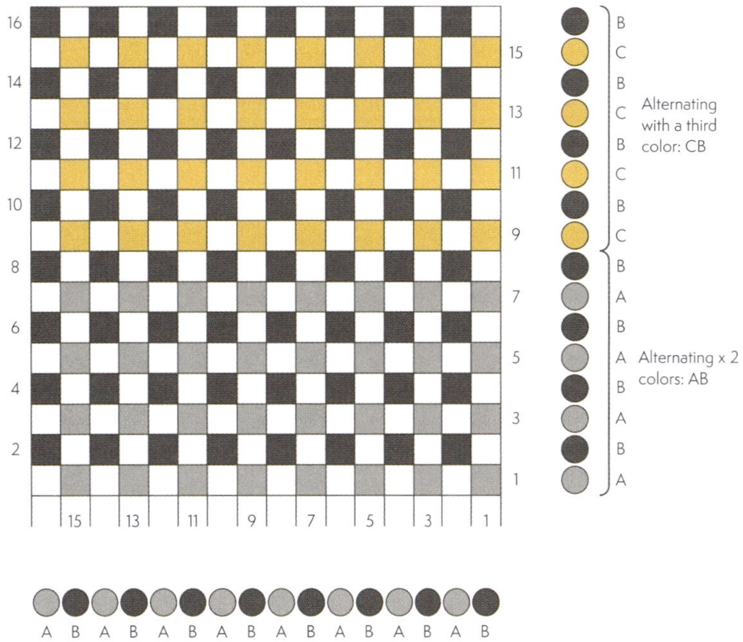

Yarn A

Yarn B

Yarn C

CHECK

The check construction consists of a series of stripes in an ordered sequence, running across both the warp and weft, and usually in the same order. The result is the very familiar design of interlacing squares and stripes, most famously associated with Scottish tartan. Woven in plain weave, the check pattern has huge design potential.

Using graph paper and colored pencils, sketch out your own design using the simple formula—draw any stripe repeat of varying thicknesses across the warp. Then repeat this stripe pattern as you weave across the weft. As so many check designs exist, you don't need to look far for inspiration, even around your own home. The number of colors that can be used in a check are endless! The more colors used, the more complex the pattern appears. This is an example of a simple check to get you started, using gray, yellow, and purple.

WEAVE CHART

This chart should be read from bottom to top, right to left.

Yarn A

Yarn B

Yarn C

Under

CHAPTER 3

THE PROJECTS

HOUNDSTOOTH SCARF

Bluefaced Leicester wool is super soft and lustrous, making it perfect to be worn next to the skin, in this case as a scarf. This project maximizes the loom's capacity to weave a long warp and create a scarf that is oversized, making it even cozier to wear. In addition, it uses a "zero waste" technique—as the ends of the warp make the fringing, the entire warp is used. Color and weave effects create the classic houndstooth pattern, woven in twill. This is punctuated with check and combined with a striped plain weave color block.

Skill level: Easy

TOOLS

Frame loom

Ten strips of cardboard, cut to the size of the warp beam: in this example, the warp beam is 9½ x ¾ in. (24 x 2 cm)

Three stick shuttles

Fork beater

Shed stick

Scissors

MATERIALS

For warp and weft

Euro / UK Brand: West Yorkshire Spinners

Yarn type: 100 percent Bluefaced Leicester wool

- **Yarn A:** Ecru 001 (Worsted) / 1.8 oz. (50 g)
- **Yarn B:** Autumn Collection—Honey 289 (Worsted) / 0.9 oz. (25 g)
- **Yarn C:** Light Brown 002 (Worsted) / 1.8 oz. (50 g)

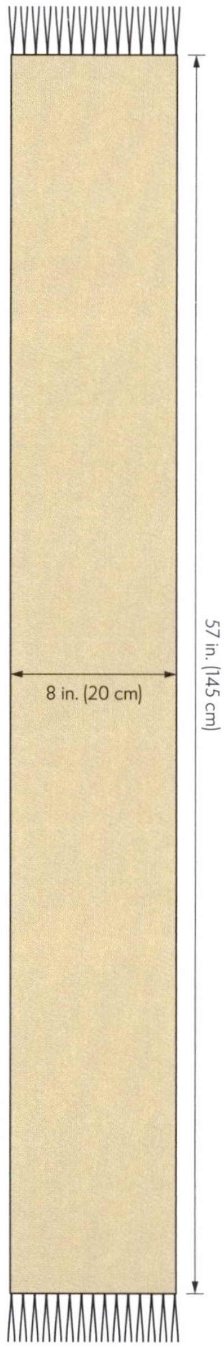

Front

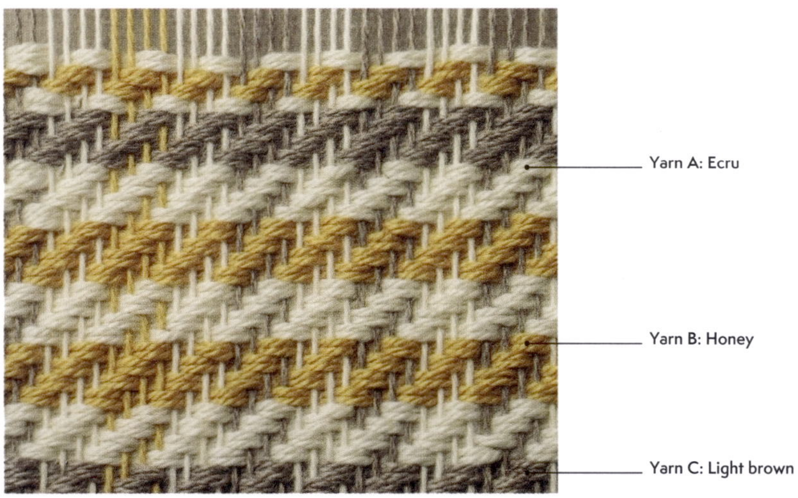

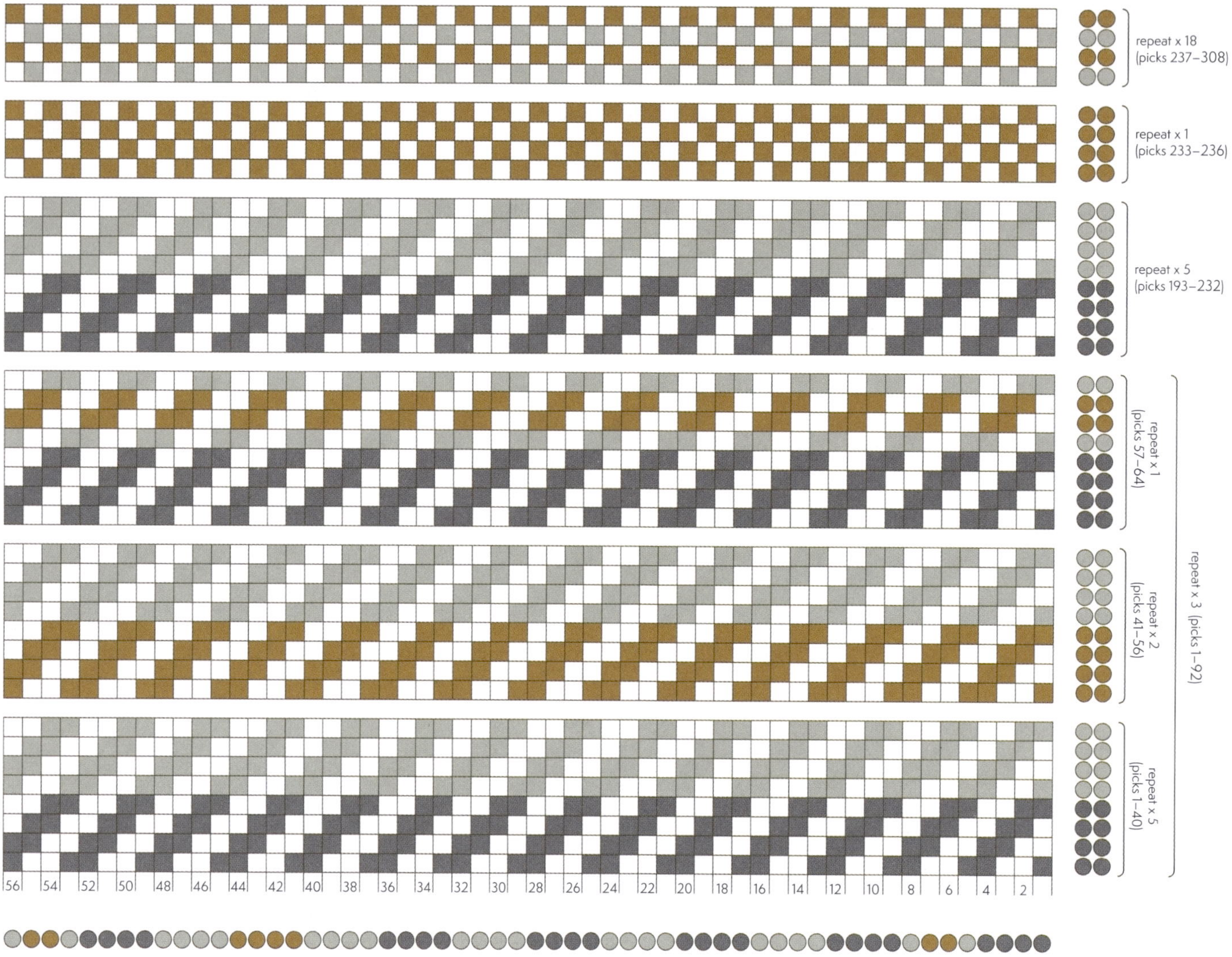

= Yarn A

= Yarn B

= Yarn C

(single dot) = Single-stranded

(double dot) = Double-stranded

SUSTAINABLE SOURCES

West Yorkshire Spinners

Based in West Yorkshire, in the heart of the original home of the British worsted spinning industry, West Yorkshire Spinners have been creating breed-specific sheep's wool yarn from British wools since 1997. They source all of their raw material locally to ensure high-quality yarns and a decreased carbon footprint, and are committed to producing wool yarn that is "reared, sheared, and spun" in Britain.

DRESSING THE LOOM

Sett: 7 ends per inch (2.5 cm)
Warp width: 8 in. (20 cm)
Total warp ends: 56
Warp length: 2.46 yd. (2.25 m)
Beat: 7 picks per inch (2.5 cm), houndstooth
9 picks per inch (2.5 cm), plain weave
Woven length: 57 in. (145 cm)

See page 30 for how to prepare a rotating (long) warp. For this project, the loom is dressed in color blocks of four threads, which along with the weft, create the twill houndstooth pattern. Begin by dressing the loom with all the warp threads in long heddles, then return to fill in the skipped warp threads in the short heddles. Follow the chart opposite for the sequence of color and yarn changes. To change warp yarn while winding, simply cut and tie in an overhand knot (see page 139) at either end of the frame loom, so that the knot lies outside the frame. Finish dressing the loom with a heading cord (see page 32).

1. The scarf features long fringing, made with the warp threads. To prepare the first fringed end, measure 8 in. (20 cm) from the beginning of the warp. Mark 8 in. (20 cm) by tying a piece of scrap yarn onto a warp thread.

2. Advance the warp, adding cardboard strips as the cloth beam rotates, until the scrap yarn sits approximately 2½ in. (6 cm) from the cloth beam. Place the heading cord here and begin weaving at this point.

1

2

THE SHUTTLES

The weft yarn is double-stranded in this design. To achieve this, wind each shuttle with two strands of the same yarn simultaneously. Then as you weave, the two strands form a single weft.

Continued overleaf.

WEAVING

Twill Houndstooth Section

1. Begin by weaving the first twill houndstooth block in Yarn C (picks 1–4). Cut and tuck the tail of Yarn C, before attaching the next shuttle with Yarn A. Weave the next four picks in Yarn A following the chart, to create the next twill houndstooth block. Repeat picks 1–8 five times (picks 1–40).

2. Continuing with the same twill weave structure, weave the next two houndstooth blocks in Yarn B (picks 41–44) and Yarn A (picks 45–48). Cut and tuck the weft tails after each houndstooth block as before. Repeat these eight picks twice (picks 41–56).

3. After weaving picks 57–60 with Yarn C, the next houndstooth block features a color change. As indicated in the chart, weave the first pick with Yarn A (pick 61). Leaving Yarn A attached, weave the next two picks with Yarn B (picks 62 and 63). Complete the block with a single pick of Yarn A (pick 64), as shown in the chart.

4. After this point, around approximately 8 in. (20 cm), the striped twill houndstooth pattern repeats. Repeat steps 1–3 three times (picks 1–192), for approximately 24 in. (61.5 cm) of woven length.

5. Weave one twill houndstooth block in Yarn C, followed by one twill houndstooth block in Yarn A (picks 193–200). Repeat these eight picks five times.

1

2

3

4

5

6

7

1/1 Plain Weave Variation Block

6. This final section of the pattern is woven entirely in plain weave structure. To begin, weave four picks using Yarn B, following the chart (picks 233–236). Then alternate each pick, weaving with Yarn B or Yarn A, as indicated in the chart. Repeat this 1/1 plain weave variation eighteen times, as shown in the chart (picks 237–308).

Finishing

7. Cut the warp threads 8 in. (20 cm) above the last woven pick and remove the piece from the loom (see page 40).

8. Once off the loom, tie the warp threads in groups of four, creating the fringing (see page 50).

8

INFINITY SCARF

This design consists of an "overshot" vertical herringbone pattern. "Overshot" refers to a pattern in which picks of plain weave (ground weft) are woven in between the desired weave structure. The effect is that the pattern really pops from the cloth! For this design, the overshot weft is double-stranded, with the ground weft single-stranded. I've used a beautiful alpaca yarn, which is silky soft with the warmth of wool—favorably comparable to cashmere fiber. What I love about this yarn is the tiny speckles of the natural, undyed fiber peeking through the colors, giving it a very full texture.

Skill level: Easy

TOOLS

Frame loom
Ten strips of cardboard, cut to the size of the warp beam; in this example, the warp beam is 9½ x ¾ in. (24 x 2 cm)
Three stick shuttles
Fork beater
Shed stick
Darning needle
Four buttons, ⅞ in. (2.25 cm) in diameter
Scissors

MATERIALS

For warp and weft

Brand: *UK Alpaca*
Yarn type: *Alpaca*

- **Yarn A:** Speckledy Gray (Bulky) / 2.5 oz. (70 g)
- **Yarn B:** Speckledy Violet (Bulky) / 2.5 oz. (70 g)
- **Yarn C:** Hot Pink (Bulky) / 2.8 oz. (80 g)*
  *Weft only

Front

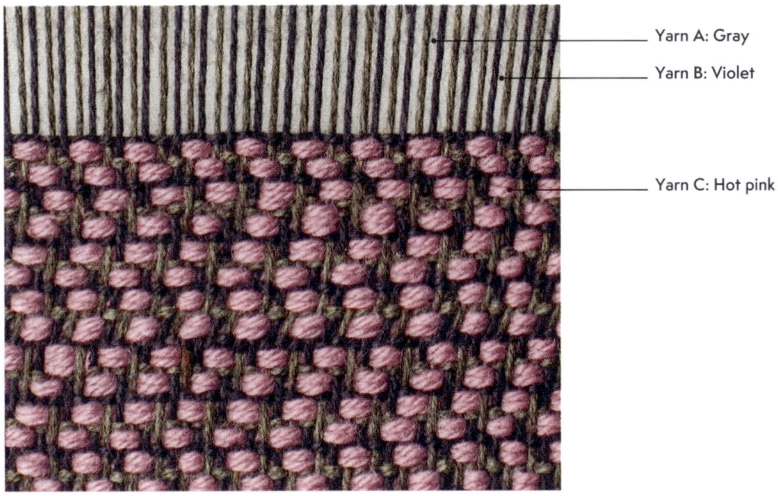

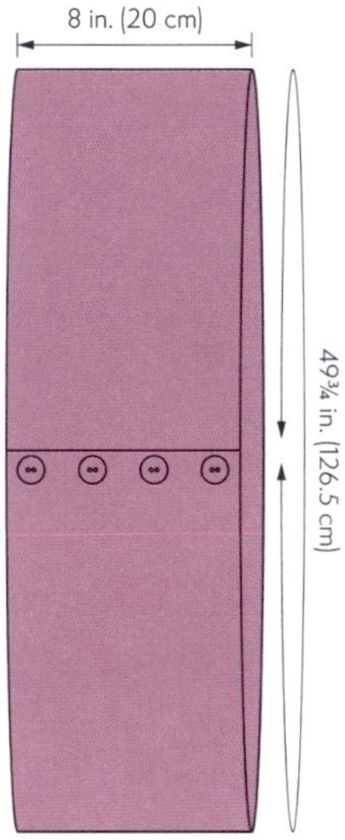

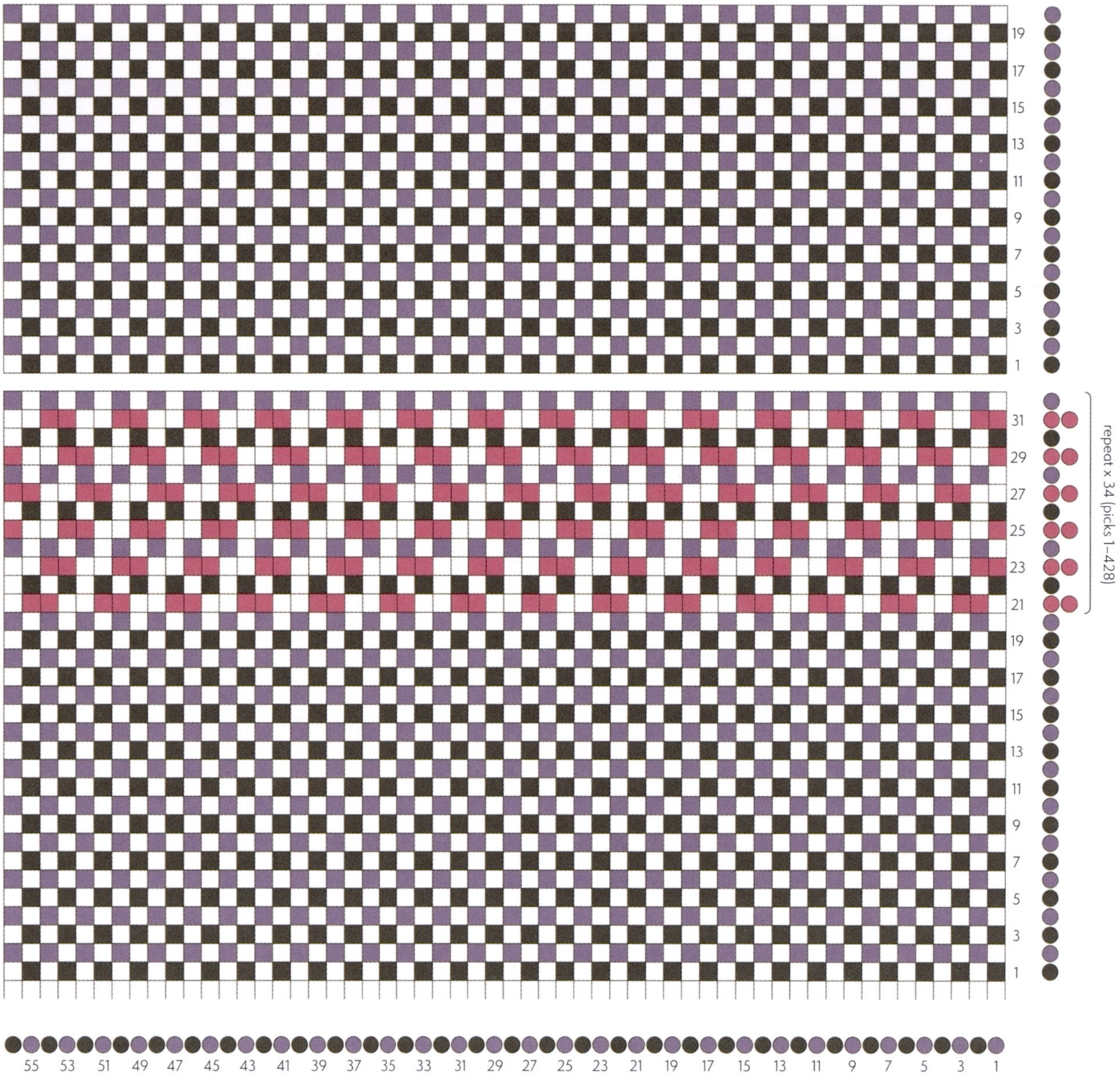

■ = Yarn A

■ = Yarn B

■ = Yarn C

● (single dot) = Single-stranded

●● (double dot) = Double-stranded

SUSTAINABLE SOURCES

UK Alpaca

UK Alpaca is run by Chas Brooke and Rachel Hebditch, alpaca farmers and breeders, who breed with a focus on the quality of both the alpacas and the fleece they yield. The largest alpaca fleece buyer in Britain, they buy more than eleven tons (11.2 tonnes) annually to produce a range of knitting and weaving yarns with full provenance. The alpaca fiber is sourced direct from farmers throughout the UK and Ireland, then all the yarn is spun in the UK.

DRESSING THE LOOM

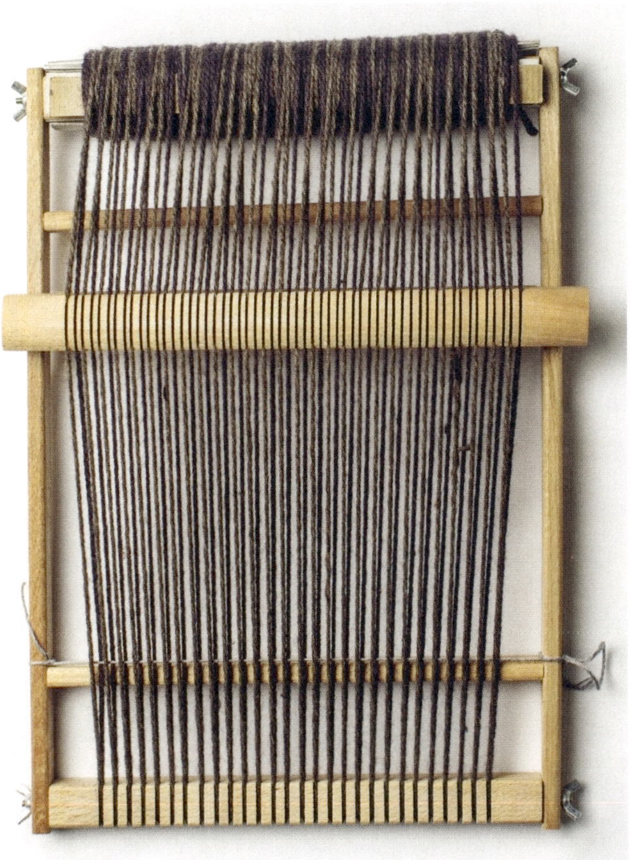

Sett: 7 ends per inch (2.5 cm)
Warp width: 8 in. (20 cm)
Total warp ends: 56
Warp length: 60 in. (150 cm)
Beat: 10 picks per inch (2.5 cm), plain weave
8 picks per inch (2.5 cm), vertical herringbone
Woven length: 49¾ in. (126.5 cm)

See page 30 for how to prepare a rotating (long) warp. For this project, the loom is dressed with a 1/1 warp, meaning the warp threads alternate on every thread between Yarn A and Yarn B. Begin by dressing the loom with all Yarn B warp threads in the long heddles, then return to fill in the skipped warp threads in the short heddles with Yarn A. Follow the chart opposite for the sequence of color and yarn changes. Finish dressing the loom with a heading cord (see page 32).

WEAVING

1. The pattern begins with a 1/1 plain weave block. Weave picks 1–20 alternate yarns, with one pick using Yarn A and one pick using Yarn B. Keep both shuttles attached as you weave, yielding around 2 in. (5 cm) of weaving.

2. From pick 21, the overshot vertical herringbone pattern begins, woven with three shuttles simultaneously. Wind the third shuttle with a double-stranded Yarn C. Following the chart, weave pick 21 with Yarn C in the first pick of the vertical herringbone weave structure. Tuck in the tail.

1

2

3

4

3. The ground weft is woven with a 1/1 plain weave, alternating Yarn A and Yarn B (similar to step one). As indicated in the chart, weave pick 22 in plain weave with Yarn A. Pick 23 is an overshot pick with Yarn C, the second pick in vertical herringbone. The image shows pick 24, the second ground-weft pick, being woven with Yarn B. Note that Yarn B weaves the opposite plain weave shed to Yarn A.

4. Continue to follow the chart to complete the overshot vertical herringbone sequence (picks 21–32), creating around 1½ in. (3.5 cm) of woven length.

5. The pattern builds by repeating this overshot vertical herringbone sequence. As indicated in the chart, repeat thirty-four times for a total of 408 picks, yielding about 47 in. (119 cm) of woven length. Measure and advance the warp as necessary, keeping the tension even to help prevent the piece from shrinking. On the last pick of Yarn C (pick 427), cut and tuck the Yarn C weft tail as you are now finished working with this yarn.

5

6

7

6. As you did in step one, finish the piece with a 1/1 plain weave block with Yarn A and Yarn B, following the chart for twenty picks to yield 1½ in. (3.5 cm) of woven length.

7. Cut the piece from the loom, leaving the warp threads at least 2½ in. (6 cm) in length, at both ends. Edge the piece at both ends with the "knot and darn" technique (see page 51).

8. Lay the two ends of the piece, right side up, next to each other. With the plain weave block you started with on top, overlap the plain weave blocks by 1½ in. (3.5 cm). Thread a darning needle with Yarn B and sew the four buttons onto the upper plain weave block at the beginning of the piece, as shown. Place the buttons ⅜ in. (1 cm) from the edge and sew at 1¼ in. (3 cm) intervals, stitching through both upper plain weave layer and lower plain weave layer.

8

MESH BAG

This project features the fabulously intricate leno weave technique (see page 46). Its open, lacelike weave creates the perfect cloth for a mesh bag. It is light and collapsible, yet stretches to fit your belongings. This project is designed with Wool and the Gang's Buddy Hemp yarn—a 55 percent hemp and 45 percent organic cotton mix yarn. Surprisingly, it handles similarly to linen, the hemp fiber giving long-lasting strength and durability, with the added bonus of being water-rot resistant. Meanwhile, the organic cotton allows the cloth to retain a very soft, light, and airy feel.

Skill level: Easy to moderate

TOOLS

Frame loom
Ten strips of cardboard, cut to the size of the warp beam; in this example, the warp beam is 11½ x 1 in. (29.25 x 2.5 cm)
Stick shuttle
Fork beater
Pick-up stick
Two temples
Darning needle
Scissors
Also: Two wooden handles, 6 in. (15 cm) wide

MATERIALS

For warp and weft
Euro / UK Brand: *Wool and the Gang*
Yarn type: *Buddy Hemp*

- **Yarn A:** Tropez Tan (Sport) / 3.5 oz. (100 g)
- **Yarn B:** Pistachio Green (Sport) / 3.5 oz. (100 g)
- **Yarn C:** Cameo Rose (Sport) / 1.75 oz. (50 g)

Front

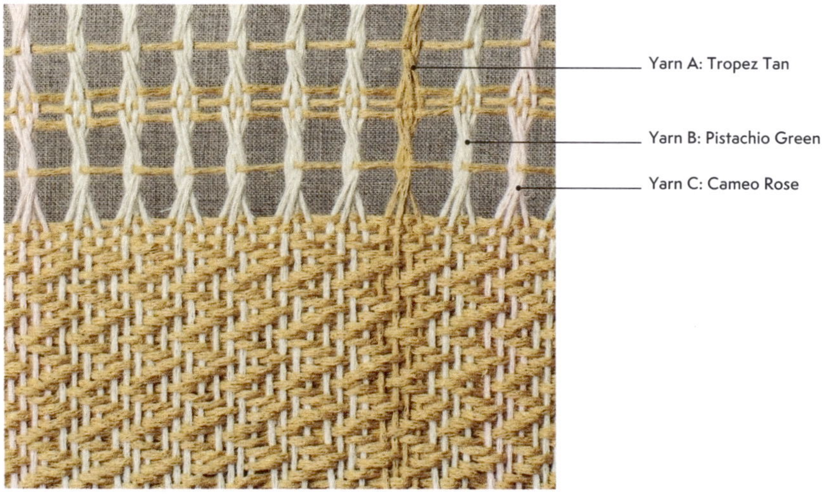

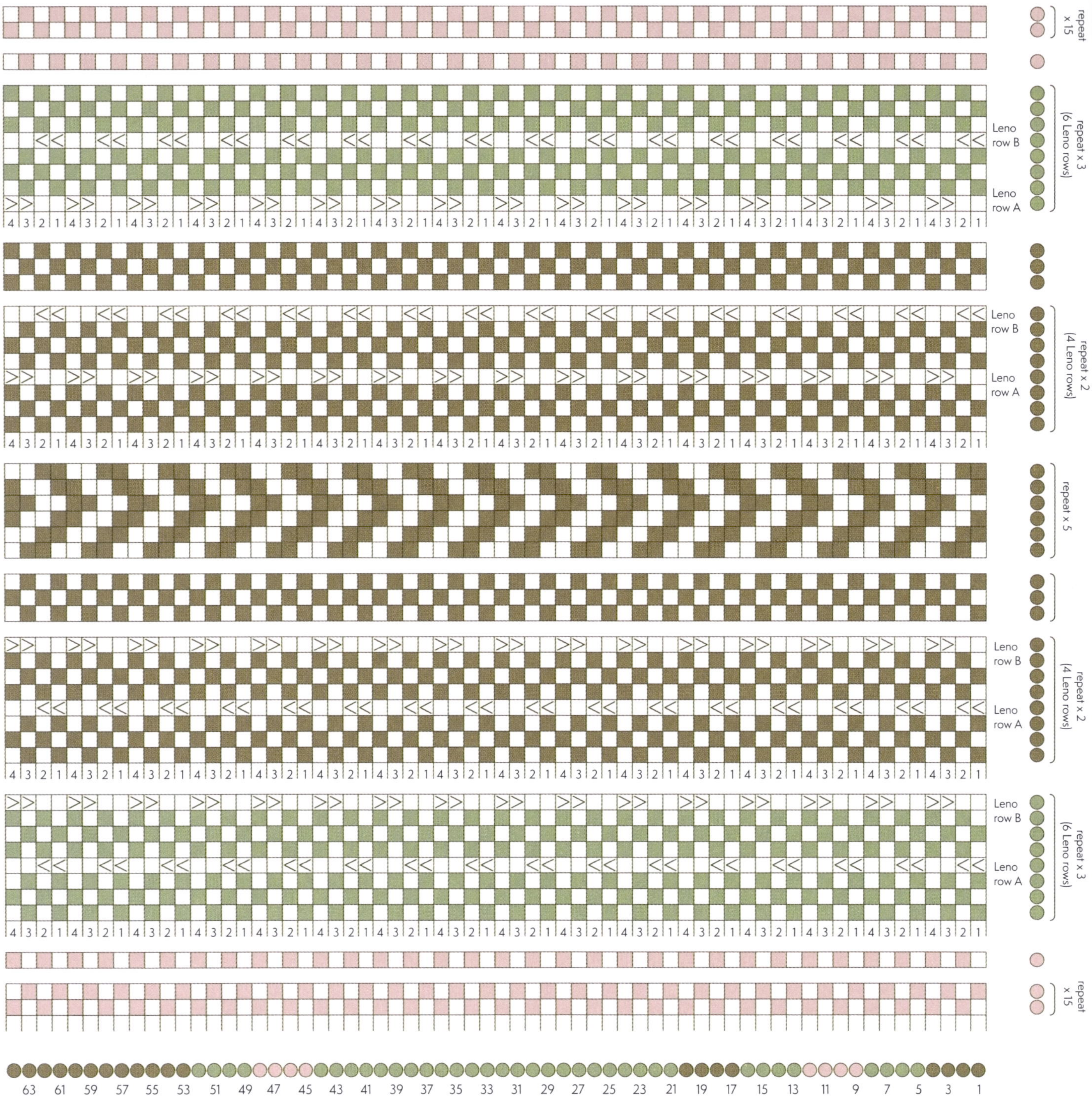

= Yarn A

= Yarn B

= Yarn C

(single dot) = Single-stranded

DRESSING THE LOOM

Sett: 6 ends per inch (2.5 cm)
Warp width: 10½ in. (26.5 cm)
Total warp ends: 64
Warp length: 43 in. (110 cm)
Beat: 15 picks per inch (2.5 cm), plain weave and vertical herringbone
8 picks per two inches (5 cm), leno weave
Woven length: 28 in. (72 cm)

See page 30 for how to prepare a rotating (long) warp. Follow the chart opposite for the sequence of color and yarn changes and count the warp threads in each color as you wind. To change warp yarn while winding, simply cut and tie in an overhand knot (see page 139) at the top of the frame loom. Finish dressing the loom with a heading cord (see page 32).

WEAVING

1. Begin by weaving 2 in. (5 cm) of plain weave with Yarn C. Beat back firmly. After weaving this block, remove the heading cord and hemstitch the beginning of the piece with Yarn C (see page 48). Make sure to weave the final pick of plain weave, as shown in the chart.

1

> **SUSTAINABLE SOURCES**
>
> **Wool and the Gang**
> Wool and the Gang is a DIY fashion brand, founded in London in 2008, powered by the global maker movement. With a strong sustainability ethos, their aim is to empower makers to create their own slow fashion through kits and yarns, all made with responsibly sourced materials, including natural, biodegradable, recycled, and vegan yarns.

Leno Blocks

2. After weaving the first three picks of the leno block in Yarn B, insert the paperclip temples into both selvages. This helps maintain the warp width.

3. Following the chart, use the pick-up stick to twist and lift the pairs of warp threads (see the leno weave instructions on page 46). Beat the weft down straight leaving a $\frac{3}{8}$ in. (1 cm) gap between the previous pick **(3a)**. Continue weaving leno in Yarn B, as per the chart. Repeat three times, making six leno rows, yielding about 7 in. (18 cm) of woven length **(3b)**. Continue to use the temple—unhooking and reattaching the paperclips in the plain weave rows as you weave. Advance the warp as necessary, keeping note of the length of your weaving as you go.

4. Wind a new shuttle with Yarn A and weave four leno rows. Complete this leno section with three picks of plain weave, as indicated in the chart.

2

3a

3b

4

5

6

Vertical Herringbone Block

5. Working with Yarn A, weave the vertical herringbone block as shown in the chart. Repeat five times, yielding around 2⅜ in. (6 cm) of woven length. Continue to beat firmly and use the temples to help maintain the weaving width.

Weaving the Reverse of the Bag

6. Following the vertical herringbone block, the pattern mirrors itself to create the reverse of the bag. Complete the next two leno blocks as before, this time with Yarn A and then Yarn B. Note that the three picks of plain weave in Yarn A occur this time between the two leno blocks. Use Yarn C for the final pick of plain weave, as shown in the chart. As you weave, beat firmly and continue measuring to keep the gaps consistent. Continue to move the temples up along the piece as you weave.

7. Finish weaving with 2 in. (5 cm) of plain weave in Yarn C, as you did at the beginning of the piece. Edge with hemstitch in Yarn C, then remove from the loom (see instructions on page 40).

7

8

Attaching the Handles

8. With reverse sides together, fold the piece in half horizontally along the center of the vertical herringbone block. If the warp fringes are quite long, trim down to approximately 2¾ in. (7 cm) from the hemstitched edge. The plain weave block at each end of the piece supports the handles. At both ends of the weaving, feed the warp fringing and ¾ in. (2 cm) of the plain weave through the slits of the wooden handles.

9. Trim down the warp tails, leaving approximately ⅜ in. (1 cm) of fringing.

10. To secure the handles, pin the edge that is folded through the handle in place and hand stitch with a backstitch, using Yarn A and a darning needle. Repeat on the other end of the weaving for the second handle.

9

Finishing

11. Fold the piece in half, using the vertical herringbone block as the center point, with reverse sides together. Graft both selvages together with Yarn A, along the right and left sides (see page 138). Finish grafting 20 ⅜ in. (8 cm) before the handle.

10

11

TOTE BAG

This project is entirely woven in the color and weave effect of log cabin (see page 62), and works best when using strongly contrasting yarns to emphasize this graphic pattern. This project is designed to be made with reclaimed or repurposed yarn from your local thrift store or your own closet! The yarns I used came from a cotton knit blanket and two knitted tops—one of which featured a metallic thread, and the other a flecked cotton. I worked the yarns as doubled-stranded to achieve a double knit (DK) weight, which is suitable for the sett of 7 ends per inch (e.p.i.) and the beat of 8.5 picks per inch (p.p.i.) The design emphasizes the curling nature of reclaimed yarns by including fringing on the bag's frontpiece. The form is constructed with two woven pieces of cloth and finished with leather handles.

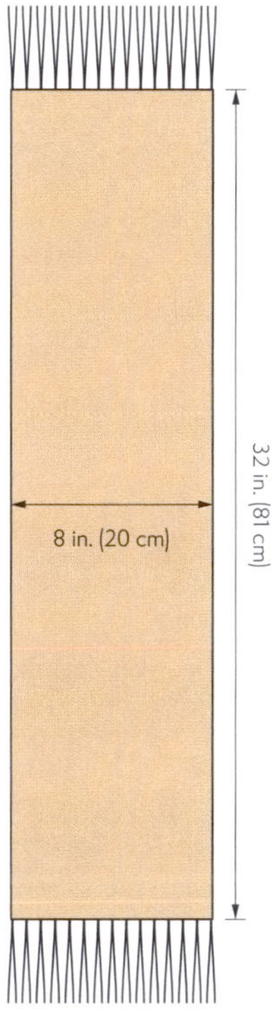

Skill level: Easy

TOOLS

Frame loom

Ten strips of cardboard, cut to the size of the warp beam; in this example, the warp beam is 9½ x ¾ in. (24 x 2 cm)

Two stick shuttles

Fork beater

Darning needle

Scissors

Also: Two handles of your choice

MATERIALS

For warp and weft

Yarn type: *Reclaimed yarn*

- **Yarn A:** Rust, cotton (DK) / 3½ oz. (100 g)
- **Yarn B:** Cream-and-gold acrylic and metallic thread (Sport) / 1¾ oz. (50 g)
- **Yarn C:** White cotton flecked with blue and purple (Sport) / 1¾ oz. (50 g)*

* Piece 2 weft only

Piece 1: Front

Piece 2: Back

Piece 1 and Piece 2 are woven on two separate (but identical) warps

Piece 2

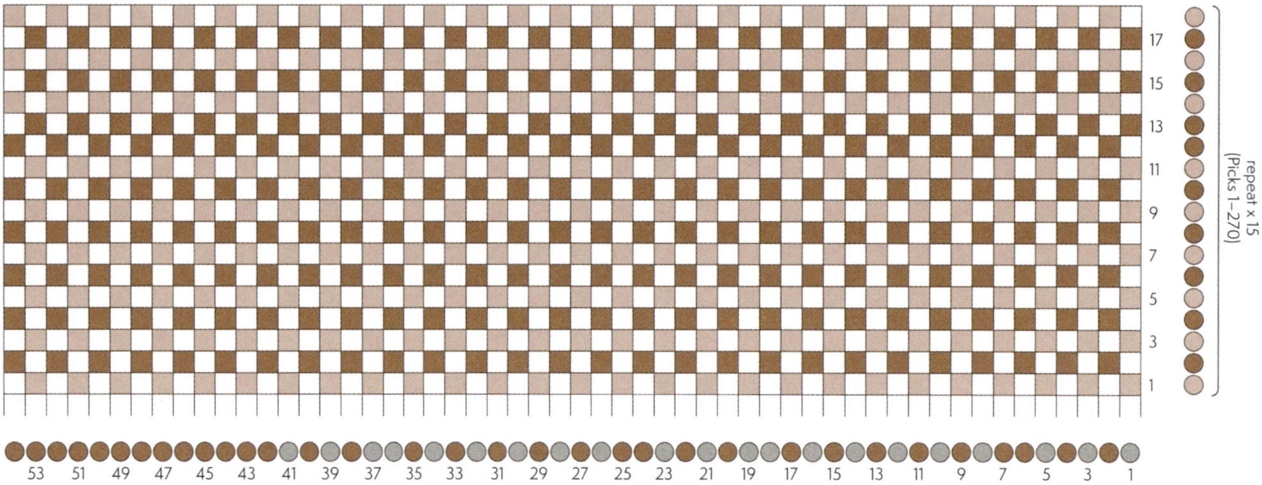

Piece 1

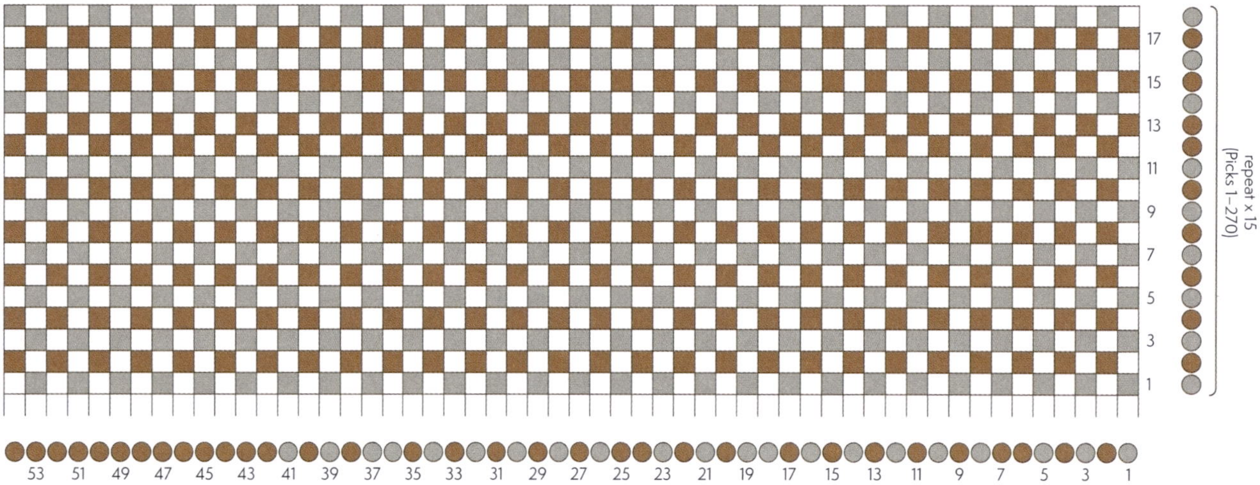

Dress the long heddles first, then the short heddles, as shown below (the blank dots represent empty heddles):

Long heddles

Short heddles

= Yarn A

= Yarn B

= Yarn C

(single dot) = Single-stranded

SUSTAINABLE SOURCES

Reclaimed Yarn

This bag is made from repurposed yarn—I found a cotton knit blanket and two knitted tops in a thrift store and unpicked them. If you have a knit garment or blanket you no longer use (but you like the yarn it is made with), turn to page 19 for instructions on how to unpick it, so the yarn can live another life and the resources used to create it are not wasted.

DRESSING THE LOOM

Sett: 7 ends per inch (2.5 cm)
Warp width: 8 in. (20 cm)
Total warp ends: 54
Warp length: 43 in. (110 cm)
Beat: 8.5 picks per inch (2.5 cm), log cabin
Woven length: 32 in. (81 cm)

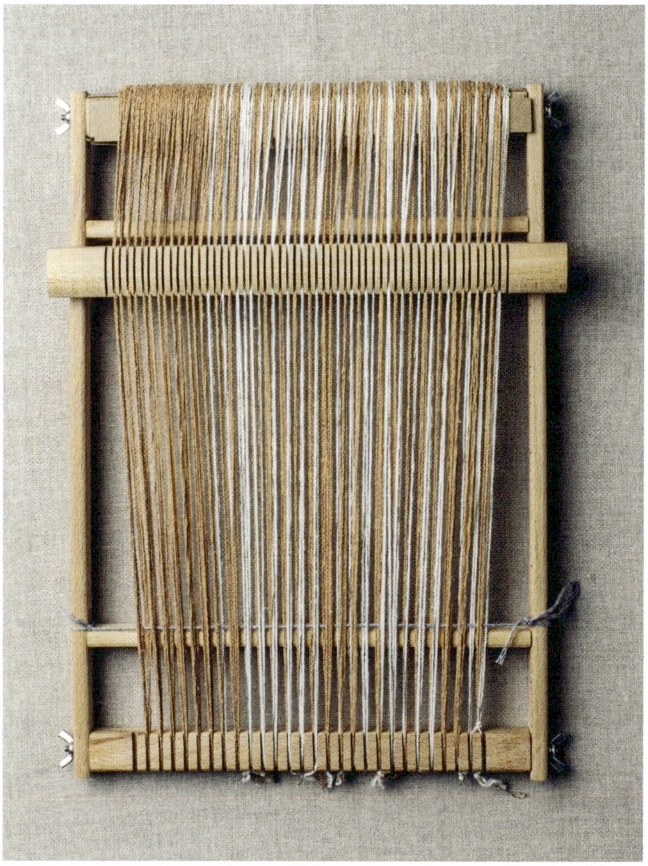

See page 30 for how to prepare a rotating (long) warp. Log cabin weave is created by the sequence of color in both the warp and weft yarns. In this design, log cabin is worked over blocks of twelve warp threads and six weft threads, where each block comprises a 1/1 warp. Follow the chart opposite to dress the loom before weaving each of the two panels.

Begin by dressing the loom with all warp threads in the long heddles, then return to fill in the skipped warp threads in the short heddles. Finish dressing the loom with a heading cord (see page 32). For the second woven piece, follow the same warp plan.

WEAVING

Piece 1

1. Weave the first section of log cabin (picks 1–12) alternating Yarn B and Yarn A six times, as shown in the chart. After weaving this section, edge with hemstitch in Yarn B (see page 48).

1

2

2. Begin the second section of log cabin (picks 13–18) with Yarn A (note the repeated weft—both pick 12 and pick 13 are woven with Yarn A) and alternate with Yarn B three times.

3. Continue weaving by repeating the log cabin sequence (picks 1–18) using Yarn A and Yarn B for fourteen sequence repeats, or until the piece measures 31½ in. (80 cm) in length. Edge with a hemstitch in Yarn B and remove from the loom (see page 40), leaving 3⅛ in. (8 cm) warp tails.

4. For the second piece of textile, dress the loom again and follow the same warp design and plan. Following the chart, weave the weft with Yarn A and Yarn C. Repeat the log cabin sequence fourteen times, or until the piece measures 31½ in. (80 cm) in length.

5. Edge with hemstitch in Yarn B and remove from the loom, leaving 3⅛ in. (8 cm) warp tails, as with Piece 1.

Continued overleaf.

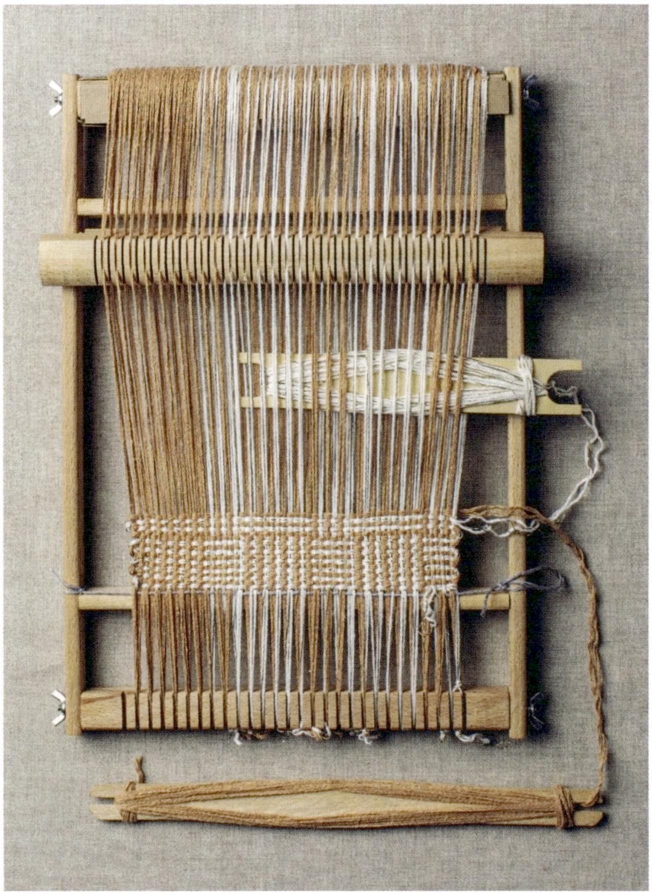

2

3

4

5

6

7

Finishing

6. Lay the two textile pieces with reverse sides together and with both the solid Yarn A warp blocks lying on top of each other. Pin together along the opposite selvage. Using a darning needle threaded with Yarn B, graft the two pieces together lengthwise on the pinned selvage (see page 138).

7. Unfold the sewn pieces, then refold in half horizontally so that both fringed edges meet. Pin in place along the hemstitched edges and sew together with a backstitch, using Yarn B.

8. You should now have a tube of woven fabric. Refold this so that the fringed edge lies vertically, down the center front of the bag. Graft the bag's front and back pieces together along the bottom edge with Yarn B. To finish, attach the handles according to the manufacturer's instructions.

8

BATH MAT

This bath mat features natural fibers of wool and nettle, woven in the intriguing waffle weave (see page 58). The yarn used in this project is a 70 percent wool and 30 percent nettle mix yarn by Onion. The nettle fiber has quick-drying properties, while the wool fibers add some bounce and coziness underfoot. As you weave, you can use the warp colors as a guide for picking up warp threads. Use the heddle bar to assist with the plain weave picks of the waffle weave structure.

Skill level: Easy to moderate

TOOLS

Frame loom*

Ten strips of cardboard, cut to the size of the warp beam; in this example, the warp beam is 9½ x ¾ in. (24 x 2 cm)

Stick shuttle

Fork beater

Pick-up stick

Two temples

Scissors

**If working on a wider frame loom, widen this warp in multiples of six threads by repeating the center warp blocks in Yarn D and Yarn A.*

MATERIALS

For warp and weft

Euro / UK Brand: *Onion*

Yarn type: *No. 6 Organic Wool and Nettle Fibers*

- **Yarn A:** Lime 624 (Worsted) / 1.8 oz. (50 g)
- **Yarn B:** Petrol 608 (Worsted) / 1.8 oz. (50 g)
- **Yarn C:** Light Green 630 (Worsted) / 1.8 oz. (50 g)*
- **Yarn D:** Light Gray 622 (Worsted) / 1.8 oz. (50 g)
- **Yarn E:** Mother of Pearl 625 (Worsted) / 1.8 oz. (50 g)**

  *Warp only

  **Weft only

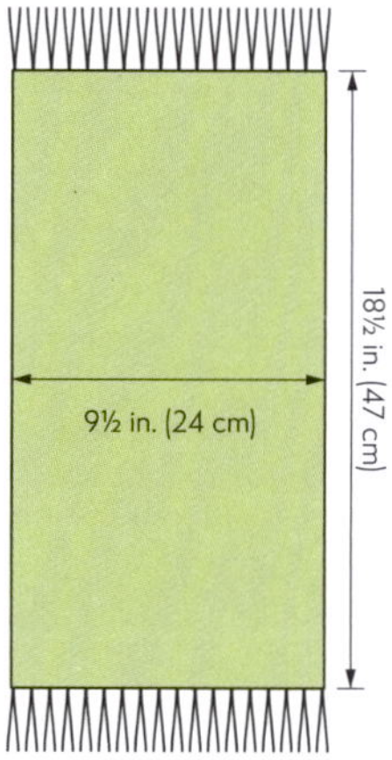

Front

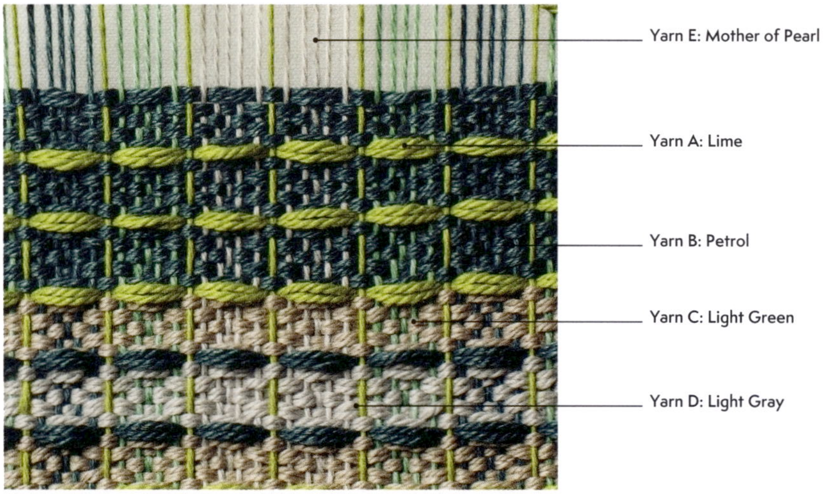

SUSTAINABLE SOURCES

Onion

Onion is a yarn company based in Denmark that uses sustainably sourced and organic fibers for their yarn collections, with an emphasis on quality, environmental responsibility, and Scandi inspiration. Their mixed yarns include materials such as camel wool, stinging nettle fibers, and tussah silk.

- Yarn A swatch = Yarn A
- Yarn B swatch = Yarn B
- Yarn C swatch = Yarn C
- Yarn D swatch = Yarn D
- Yarn E swatch = Yarn E
- (single dot) = Single-stranded
- (double dot) = Double-stranded

DRESSING THE LOOM

Sett: 6 ends per inch (2.5 cm)
Warp width: 10½ in. (26.5 cm)
Total warp ends: 64
Warp length: 35½ in. (90 cm)
Beat: 16 picks per inch (2.5 cm), plain and waffle weave
Woven length: 18½ in. (47 cm)

See page 30 for how to prepare a rotating (long) warp, and follow the chart on pages 102–103 for the sequence of color and yarn changes. To change warp yarn while winding, simply cut and tie in an overhand knot at either end of the frame loom so that the knot lies outside the frame (see page 139). Make sure to count the warp threads in each color as you wind so that you have the correct amount of yarn per color for the waffle. Finish dressing the loom with a heading cord (see page 32).

WEAVING

1. Once you have woven the first two picks of plain weave using double-stranded Yarn D, the first waffle block begins. Leaving Yarn D attached, insert one pick of Yarn A, weaving the waffle float pick. Then continue the waffle weave block in Yarn D (up to pick 8). Finish Yarn D at this point and tuck in the tail.

2. At this point, edge the beginning of the piece with hemstitch (see page 48).

3. After weaving the next waffle float (pick 9) in Yarn A, the next waffle block begins. This time it is woven with a double-stranded Yarn E. Weave picks 10–14 with Yarn E, as shown in the chart. Complete the waffle with a float pick using Yarn B (pick 15).

4. Continue weaving, alternating waffle blocks with Yarn D and Yarn E. Refer to the chart for the yarn color of the waffle float picks (Yarn A or Yarn B) until pick 39.

5. For picks 40–57, the waffle weave blocks are woven using Yarn B, with the float picks woven with Yarn A. Repeat three times, as indicated in the chart.

1

2

3

4

5

6

6. Follow the chart to weave the alternating waffle weave blocks in Yarn D and Yarn E. Weave the waffle float picks in either Yarn A or Yarn B, as shown in the chart. While weaving, advance the warp as necessary and trim any tails. Pay particular attention to your selvages and ensure you make a weft arc as you weave to prevent too much shrinkage.

7. Finish the last pick with a hemstitch edge (see page 48), using a single strand of Yarn D.

Finishing

8. Remove from the loom by cutting the warp threads horizontally, 2 in. (5 cm) above the top hemstitched edge **(8a)**. Take the piece from the loom and cut the warp threads horizontally at the bottom hemstitched edge **(8b)**.

7

8a

8b

TABLE RUNNER

In this project, the pattern is created through the placement of color, which in weaving is referred to as "color and weave" effect. As such, this is an easy weave as it is woven entirely in plain weave structure. Woven with a beautifully crisp linen yarn, it is highly durable and perfectly functional while decorating any table. As this yarn is a fine fingering weight, for this project I have woven multiple strands together to increase its weight—and the result is fabulous!

Skill level: Easy

TOOLS

Frame loom
Ten strips of cardboard, cut to the size of the warp beam; in this example, the warp beam is 8¾ x ¾ in. (22 x 2 cm)
Stick shuttle
Fork beater
Pick-up stick
Scissors

MATERIALS

For warp and weft

Brand: *BC Garn*

Yarn type: *Lino (Linen)*

- **Yarn A:** Dark Chocolate LN32 (Fingering) / 1.8 oz. (50 g)*
- **Yarn B:** Amber LN36 (Fingering) / 1.8 oz. (50 g)
- **Yarn C:** Natural LN33 (Fingering) / 1.8 oz. (50 g)

* Warp only

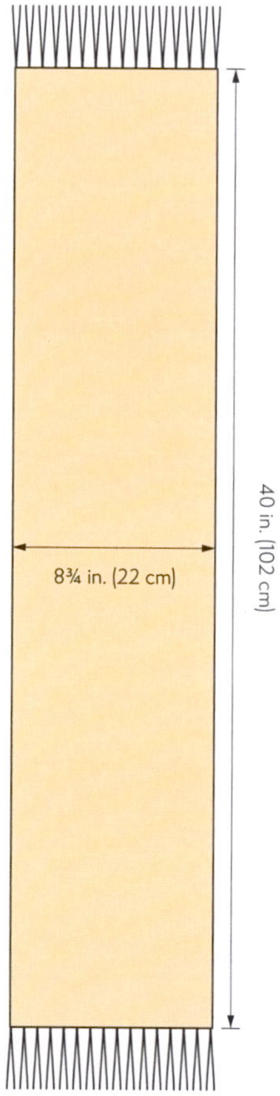

Front

■ = Yarn A

■ = Yarn B

■ = Yarn C

●● (double dot) = Double-stranded

●●● (triple dot) = Triple-stranded

185
183
181
179
177
175
173
171
169
167
165
163
161
159
157
155
153
151
149
147
145
143
141
139
137
135
133
131
129
127
125
123
121
119
117
115
113
111
109
107
105
103
101
99
97
95
93
91
89
87
85

Midway point of pattern (see step 7)

371
369
367
369
365
363
361
359
357
355
353
351
349
347
347
345
343
341
339
337
335
333
331
329
327
325
323
321
319
317
315
311
309
307
303
301
299
297
295
293
291
289

DRESSING THE LOOM

Sett: 7 ends per inch (2.5 cm)
Warp width: 8 in. (20 cm)
Total warp ends: 56
Warp length: 47¼ in. (120 cm)
Beat: 9 picks per inch (2.5 cm), plain weave
Woven length: 40 in. (102 cm)

See page 30 for how to prepare a rotating (long) warp. This warp is double-stranded, so it involves an extra step when setting up the loom. First, wind all warp threads in the long heddles with a single thread, skipping the short heddles. Begin by winding one thread of Yarn A, cut and tie onto Yarn B, winding all Yarn B threads (ending on the second last dent). Cut and retie Yarn A for a single thread. Repeat this so all warp threads are double-stranded. Now wind the alternate warp threads in the short heddles, using the same method and following the color sequence in the chart.

THE SHUTTLES

The weft yarn is triple-stranded in this design. To achieve this, wind each shuttle with three strands of the same yarn simultaneously. Then as you weave, the three strands will form a single weft.

1

SUSTAINABLE SOURCES

BC Garn
BC Garn is a Danish yarn brand originally founded in 1972 that prides itself on being the brand with the most yarns certified by the Global Organic Textile Standard (GOTS) in the industry. Their yarns are always made from natural fibers and are often organic. Their lino yarn featured in this project is 100 percent European linen, grown from flax plants in Italy then spun and dyed in Serbia. The yarn is rustic yet lustrous and is beautifully soft.

2

3

WEAVING

1. After dressing the loom, begin by weaving ten picks of plain weave in a solid color block with Yarn B, yielding approximately 1¼ in. (3 cm) of woven length.

2. Keeping the Yarn B shuttle attached, a second shuttle with Yarn C is now introduced. Follow the chart to weave one pick with Yarn C, followed by three picks with Yarn B. Repeat this sequence nine times from picks 11–46, resulting in approximately 4 in. (10 cm) of woven length.

3. Picks 47–83 form the border section, where Yarn C is dominant, yielding approximately 4 in. (10 cm) of woven length. Begin the border by weaving a 2/1 block (repeat two picks in Yarn C followed by one pick in Yarn B) five times, until pick 61.

4. Continuing the border from pick 62, weave a 1/1 block (one pick in Yarn B, followed by one pick in Yarn C) four times, until pick 69. Follow this with five blocks of 2/1 (see step three), until pick 84.

Continued overleaf.

4

5

6

5. The next section is picks 85–152, woven as a 3/1 block (three picks in Yarn B, followed by one pick in Yarn C—see step 1). Note that Yarn C is now woven on the opposite plain weave shed as before, creating a new pattern. Repeat seventeen times to yield approximately 7 in. (18 cm) of woven length.

6. Following the chart, weave pick 153 in Yarn C before weaving the center section as a 2/2 block (two picks in Yarn B, followed by two picks in Yarn C) sixteen times, yielding approximately 7½ in. (19 cm) of woven length. To finish this section, weave two picks in Yarn B.

7. The 2/2 block at pick 186 is the center of the table runner, so now you are beginning to mirror the sections from the first half, which gives the runner its symmetrical design. Continue from pick 220, following the chart closely to ensure the correct placement of colors. After repeating the 3/1 block seventeen times (and the border section), the pattern ends with a 3/1 block on the opposite shed, followed by a solid block of Yarn B. This takes you to the final pick (371).

Finishing

8. Remove the piece from the loom (see page 40), making sure you cut the warp threads at least 3¼ in. (8 cm) from the weaving. Edge with overhand knot fringing (see page 50).

7

8

TASSELED PILLOW

This project is filled with so much texture. It features raised surface decoration of vertical soumak braids (see page 44) and extra-weft tassels combined. Woven as one piece, the resulting cloth forms an envelope-style pillow that allows for minimal sewing and zero waste. All the yarns used in this design are from West Yorkshire Spinners' Croft collection, which is produced from 100 percent Shetland Island wool. Known for its durability yet surprising softness, this yarn helps make a perfect pillow for your home. I particularly love the tweed colorways in this yarn collection.

Skill level: Easy to moderate

TOOLS

Frame loom

Ten strips of cardboard, cut to the size of the warp beam; in this example, the warp beam is 9½ x ¾ in. (24 x 2 cm)

Thee stick shuttles

Fork beater

Shed stick

Darning needle

Scissors

Also: Pillow insert, 13½ x 9 in. (33.5 x 23 cm)

MATERIALS

For warp and weft

Euro / UK Brand: West Yorkshire Spinners

Yarn type: The Croft (Shetland wool tweed)

- **Yarn A:** Clousta (Worsted) / 3½ oz. (100 g)
- **Yarn B:** Lerwick (Worsted) / 3½ oz. (100 g)
- **Yarn C:** Melby (Worsted) / 3½ oz. (100 g)
- **Yarn D:** Dark Brown (Worsted) / 3½ oz. (100 g)
- **Yarn E:** Huxter (Worsted) / 3½ oz. (100 g)
- **Yarn F:** Hillswick (Worsted) / 3½ oz. (100 g)

Front

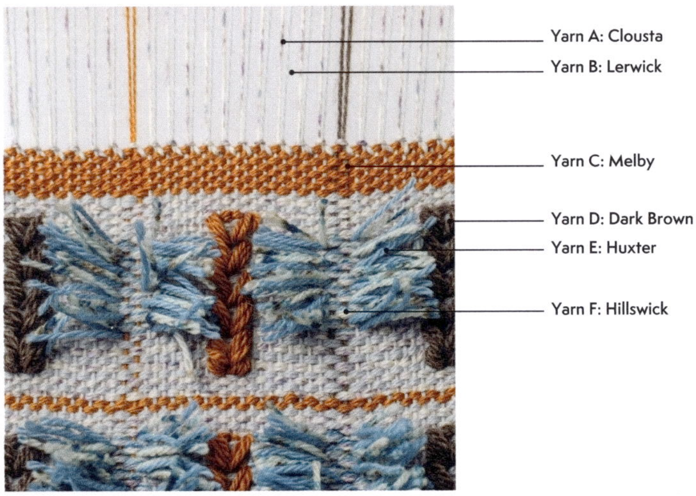

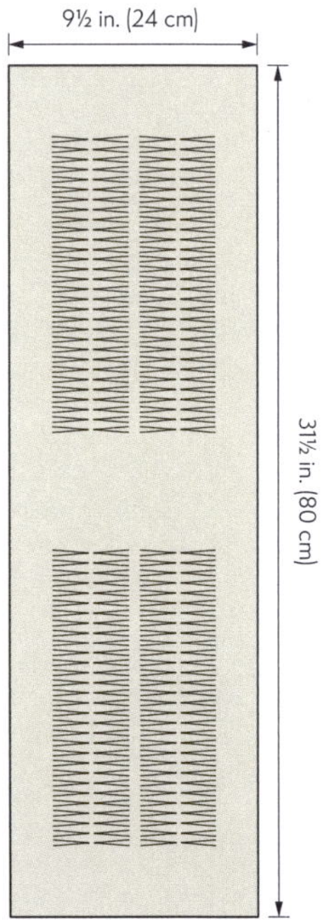

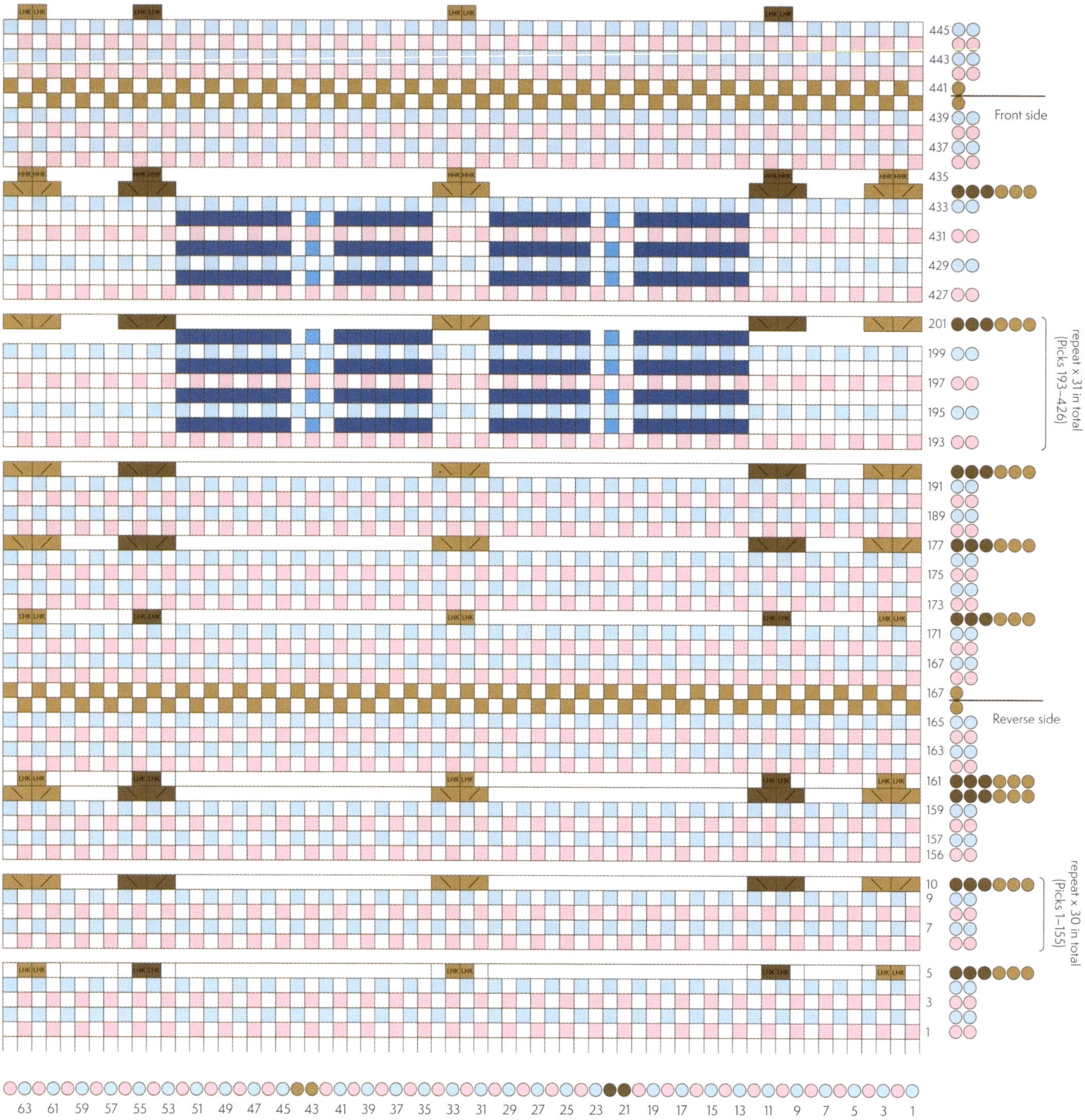

= Yarn A

= Yarn B

= Yarn C

= Yarn D

= Yarn E and F

Float (Yarns E and F)

Extra-weft: woven (Yarns E and F)

(single dot) = Single-stranded

(double dot) = Double-stranded

(triple dot) = Triple-stranded

Soumak stitch

LHK Lark's head knot

HHK Half hitch knot

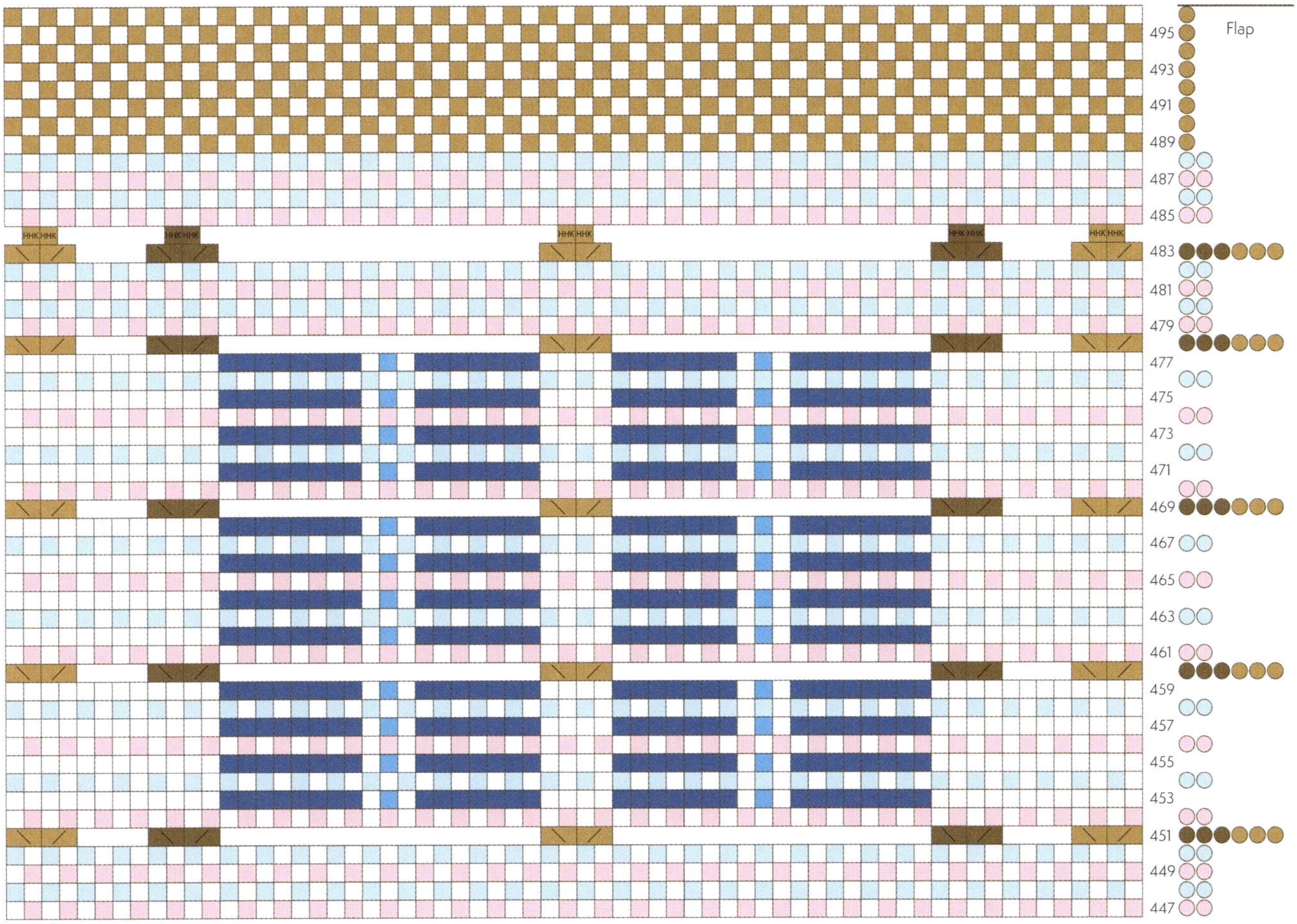

DRESSING THE LOOM

Sett: 6 ends per inch (2.5 cm)
Warp width: 10½ in. (26.5 cm)
Total warp ends: 64
Warp length: 43 in. (110 cm)
Beat: 7 picks per inch (2.5 cm), plain weave, plus vertical soumak and tassels
Woven length: 31½ in. (80 cm)

See page 30 for how to prepare a rotating (long) warp. For this project, the loom is dressed mainly with a 1/1 warp (Yarn A and Yarn B), including two-color stripes (Yarn C and Yarn D). These stripes form the backbone for the extra-weft tassels on the front and flap of the pillow. Begin by dressing the loom with all warp threads in the long heddles, then return to fill in the skipped warp threads in the short heddles. Finish dressing the loom with a heading cord (see page 32).

1

WEAVING

Reverse Side

1. Weave four picks in plain weave, alternating Yarn A and Yarn B (double-stranded). Wind six finger skeins of triple-stranded Yarn C and four fingers skeins of triple-stranded Yarn D. Attach to the warp threads with lark's head knots (see page 139), as indicated in the chart on pages 120–121.

2. After weaving four more picks in plain weave, alternating Yarn A and Yarn B, weave the first row of vertical soumak with each finger skein.

3. Continue weaving the vertical soumaks at four-pick intervals and see the braids build up. Repeat this sequence—four plain weave picks, plus one vertical soumak row—thirty-one times in total, as shown in the chart. After the final vertical soumak pick, tuck in the weft tail and pull it through to the reverse side (pick 162).

4. After finishing the vertical soumak, weave four picks of plain weave alternating in Yarn A and Yarn B. This completes the reverse side of the pillow cover. Weave two picks in Yarn C. You should have 14¾ in. (37.5 cm) of woven length.

2

3

4

5

6

Front Side

5. To begin weaving the front side of the pillow cover, repeat step one. Then repeat step two—completing four picks of plain weave, plus one vertical soumak row—a total of four times, as shown in the chart. After the fourth vertical soumak, extra-weft tassels begin. Follow the chart closely to weave one pick with Yarn A, and one extra-weft pick with Yarns E and F. Then weave one pick with Yarn B, and one extra-weft pick with Yarns E and F. Next, weave one extra-weft pick with Yarns E and F in between each plain weave pick (Yarn A or Yarn B). Beat each row down firmly.

6. Once you have woven pick 200, make two cuts in the extra weft float on each side of the central vertical soumak braid. Weave the next row of vertical soumak with each finger skein at pick 201, as before.

7. Continue weaving this sequence—one extra-weft pick with Yarns E and F in between each plain weave pick (Yarn A or Yarn B); weave one vertical soumak row after every fourth extra-weft pick. Beat firmly. After weaving thirty-one vertical soumaks in total on the front side, tie off all the finger skeins with a half hitch knot (see page 139). Finish the front side with four picks of plain weave in Yarn A and B, followed by two picks in Yarn C, as per the chart. At pick 441, you should have another 14¾ in. (37.5 cm) of woven length to match the back of the pillow.

7

Weaving the Flap

8. Follow the chart to weave the flap, using vertical soumak braids and extra-weft tassels, as instructed in step seven and following the chart. Finish the piece with eight picks of plain weave with Yarn C—you should have a flap measuring 4 in. (10 cm). Edge the weaving with a hemstitch (see page 48), using a single strand of Yarn A. Remove from the loom and trim the warp tails to ⅜ in. (1 cm) in length (see page 40).

8

Sewing Up

9. To hem the flap, place the piece reverse side up, folding the Yarn C block in half (four picks folded over four picks). Press with an iron and pin in place. Using a single strand of Yarn C, backstitch across the hem to hold it in place.

9

10. Lay the piece flat, reverse side up, with the hemmed Yarn C block at the top. From the bottom, fold the piece along the first two Yarn C wefts so that the reverse sides are together. Fold down the flap along the second two Yarn C wefts, with the right side facing up. Pin both selvages together along the sides, including the flap **(10a)**. Graft along both selvages (see page 138), with a single-stranded length of Yarn A, as shown **(10b)** .

Pin the cover along both selvages, including the closed flap.

10a Full reverse side of pillow

Graft the selvages together, including the closed flap.

10b Full front side of pillow

BOLSTER PILLOW

This fun design features the pinwheel weave (see page 60), combined with plain weave and a subtle check (see page 66), with added extra-weft bows (see page 42). The cover is woven as two pieces and constructed using reclaimed upholstery fabric for the ends. The shelter and quarry yarns used in this design are made using wool from the Targhee and Columbia breeds of sheep. The Arbor yarn, used in the mustard accent, is made with pure Targhee sheep's wool from Montana and South Dakota.

Skill level: Easy to moderate

TOOLS

Frame loom
Ten strips of cardboard, cut to the size of the warp beam; in this example, the warp beam is 11½ x 1 in. (29.25 x 2.5 cm)
Stick shuttle
Fork beater
Pick-up stick
Two temples
Darning needle
Scissors
Also: Reclaimed upholstery fabric, 15¾ x 8 in. (40 x 20 cm)
Bolster insert, 18½ x 6 in. (47 x 15 cm)

MATERIALS

For warp and weft
US Brand: Brooklyn Tweed
Yarn type: See individual yarns

- **Yarn A:** Shelter Woodsmoke (Worsted) / 1¾ oz. (50 g)
- **Yarn B:** Shelter Plume (Worsted) / 1¾ oz. (50 g)
- **Yarn C:** Shelter Flannel (Worsted) / 1¾ oz. (50 g)
- **Yarn D:** Quarry Citrine (Bulky) / 3½ oz. (100 g)
- **Yarn E:** Quarry Sandstone (Bulky) / 3½ oz. (100 g)*
- **Yarn F:** Arbor Klimt (DK) / 1¾ oz. (50 g)*

* Weft only

Front

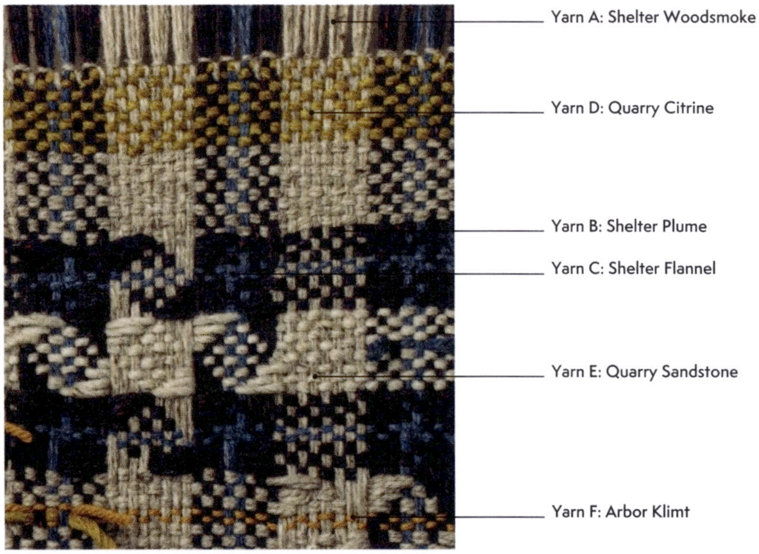

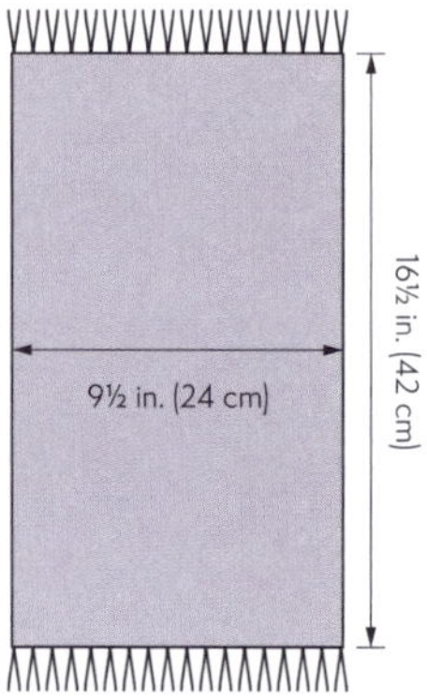

Woven as two pieces of the same warp and weft design

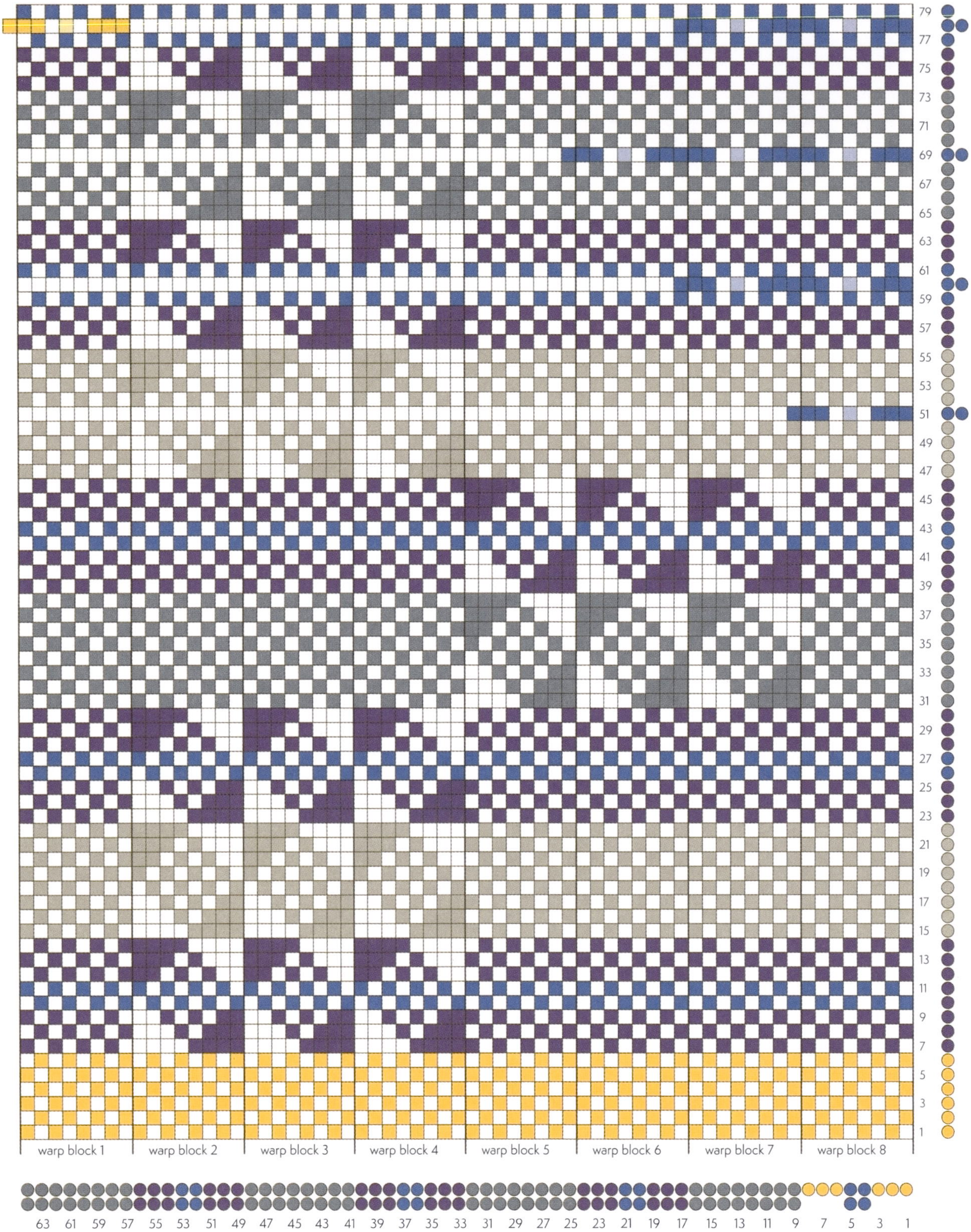

■ = Yarn A

■ = Yarn B

■ = Yarn C

■ = Yarn D

■ = Yarn E

■ = Yarn F

● (single dot) = Single-stranded

●● (double dot) = Double-stranded

■ Float (Yarn C)

■ Extra-weft: woven (Yarn C)

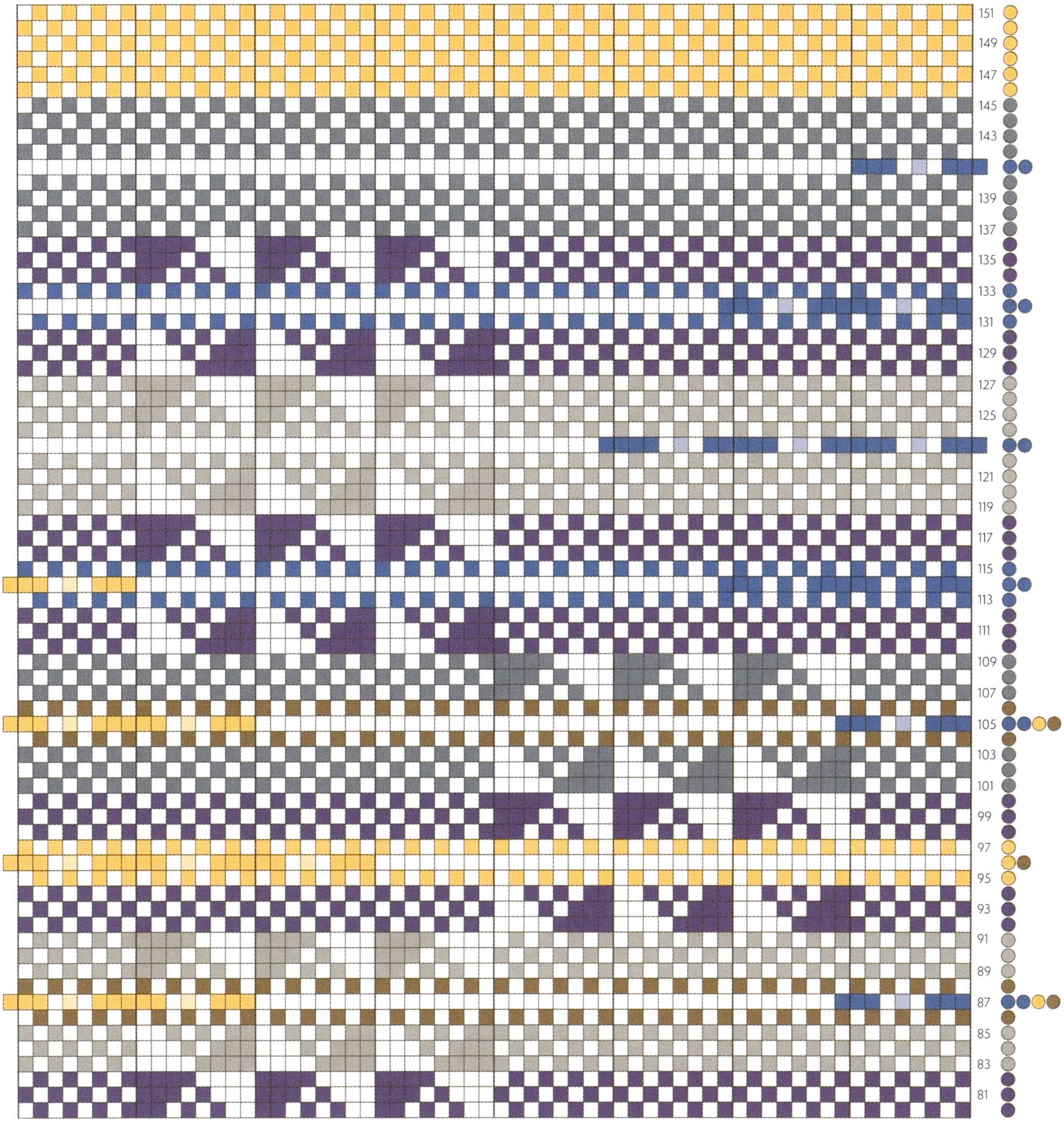

SUSTAINABLE SOURCES

Brooklyn Tweed

Brooklyn Tweed was founded in 2005 by Jared Flood as a blog for knitters. The company grew into a maker of sustainable, breed-specific American yarn and is now a standard-setting knitting design house. Specializing in wool yarns, the product they develop and manufacture is 100 percent local, fortifying the United States fiber supply chain from sheep to skein.

WEAVING

1. After weaving six picks of plain weave—approximately 1 in. (2.5 cm) of woven length—with Yarn D, the first pinwheel block begins. In this design, the pinwheel is woven over three warp blocks, with the remaining three warp blocks in plain weave. Following the chart, weave pinwheel on blocks two, three, and four. To begin, weave the first block with Yarn B, using Yarn C for the center two picks (10 and 11). At this point, edge the beginning of the piece with a hemstitch (see page 48), using a single strand of Yarn A. Weave the next pinwheel block with Yarn E only and see the pinwheel emerge. Then go on to weave the next pinwheel block, again using Yarn B and Yarn C (picks 23–30).

2. Once you have finished weaving the first pinwheel (picks 7–30), the placement of the pinwheel shifts to the right-hand side and is now woven over warp blocks five, six, and seven (picks 31–46). Follow the chart to weave a pinwheel alongside plain weave in Yarn A, then weave the central block using Yarn B and Yarn C.

DRESSING THE LOOM

Sett: 6 ends per inch (2.5 cm)
Warp width: 10½ in. (26.5 cm)
Total warp ends: 64
Warp length: 35½ in. (90 cm)
Beat: 8 picks per inch (2.5 cm), plain weave and pinwheel
Woven length: 16½ in. (42 cm)

See page 30 for how to prepare a rotating (long) warp. The pinwheel pattern is woven over blocks of eight warp threads, making this warp striped. For the warp, all Yarn A, Yarn B, and Yarn C warp threads are double-stranded. Begin by winding all Yarn A warp threads—wind two strands of Yarn A in the first four long heddles, skip the next four long heddles and repeat across the frame until you have four blocks of Yarn A. Next, fill in the skipped long heddles with Yarn B and Yarn C for the alternate warp stripes, as shown in the chart on pages 128–129. For the final stripe, replace Yarn B with Yarn D (single-stranded). Once all the long heddles are filled, wind all the warp threads in the short heddles using the same method. Finish dressing the loom with a heading cord (see page 32).

1

2

3

3. On the next pinwheel block (picks 47–55) woven with Yarn E, the extra-weft bows begin. Weave pick 51, the first extra-weft pick, with Yarn C, as indicated in the chart, creating one extra-weft bow (see page 42). Continue weaving as per the chart. Weave the next extra-weft row (pick 60) with Yarn C, as shown in the chart, creating two extra-weft bows this time. You should now have 7⅜ in. (18.75 cm) of woven length on the loom.

4

4. Continue weaving, following the chart. Pick 78 marks the beginning of the Yarn D and Yarn F extra-weft bow blocks. Note that this overlaps with the end of the Yarn C extra-weft bows until pick 87.

5. In this next section, note the extra-weft bows in Yarn D and Yarn F are coupled with the Yarn D and Yarn F wefts at the center points of the pinwheels (picks 86–109). Finish the Yarn D and Yarn F extra-weft bow section on pick 114.

5

6

6. You should now have 19¾ in. (50 cm) of woven length on the loom. Complete the weave, as per the chart, and edge with a hemstitch using a single strand of Yarn A. Remove from the loom by trimming the warp tails 1 in. (2.5 cm) above the hemstitched edge.

7. Repeat steps 1–6 to weave an identical second piece.

Finishing

8. Lay the two woven pieces with reverse sides together, aligning Yarn D and Yarn F wefts with Yarn D extra-weft bows. Using a darning needle (threaded with a single strand of Yarn A), graft the two pieces together along one selvage so that the Yarn D and Yarn F extra-weft bows meet and align (see page 138).

9. From the reclaimed upholstery fabric, cut two circles, each 7 in. (18 cm) in diameter. A side plate makes a suitable template.

10. Working with the reverse side up (of both the woven cloth and circles), lay one circle of upholstery fabric over one end of the woven piece, so that the edge of the circle covers the Yarn D plain weave block. Pin the circle in place ⅜ in. (1 cm) in from the hemstitched woven edge. Continue rotating the fabric circle to line up with the first Yarn D pick (pick 146), pinning as you rotate.

8

9

10

11

11. Once pinned halfway, start to stitch the circle of fabric in place using a backstitch and a single strand of Yarn A. Make sure to sew along the hemstitched edge, leaving the warp fringing free on the outside.

12. Repeat steps ten and eleven on the second half of the woven piece so that the entire circumference of the circle is sewn in place. Where the two woven edges meet, overlap by 1 in. (2.5 cm) and sew together. Using the second circle of fabric, repeat at the opposite end of the pillow.

The pillow cover should now form a cylinder with a flap opening lengthwise. Insert the pillow pad.

12

MAKING YOUR OWN FRAME LOOM

TOOLS

Metric ruler*
Imperial ruler (optional)
Graphite pencil
Colored pencil
Masking tape
Knife saw
Sandpaper
Drill
Wrench

MATERIALS

¾ x ¾ in. (2 x 2 cm) square dowels in the following lengths:
- Two measuring 11¾ in. (30 cm)
- Two measuring 15¾ in. (40 cm)
- One measuring 13⅝ in. (34.5 cm)

Four wing nuts (M8)
Four washers (M8)
Four bolts (woodscrew to machine thread screw), M8 x 3 in. (7.5 cm)

Making the Warp and Cloth Beam

1. On one of the 11¾ in. (30 cm) dowel pieces, measure 1 in. (2.5cm) from both ends and mark with the pencil. Repeat on the second 11¾ in. (30 cm) dowel.

2. Firmly tape the two dowels together lengthwise at either end, between the pencil marks and the end of the dowels.

3. Use the ruler and pencil to mark ¼ in. (7 mm) increments between the 1 in. (2.5 cm) marks at both ends as shown, across both dowels.

4. With the knife saw, cut into each marking 3⁄16 in. (5 mm) deep to create dents.

5. Sand down the cuts to smooth the edges. Remove the tape to separate the dowels (these will become your warp and cloth beams).

4

IMPORTANT

The dents on this loom are spaced at ¼ in. (7 mm) increments. When measuring these dents, it is best to use a metric ruler to ensure precise results.

This will create an overall sett of 7 e.p.i., which is the e.p.i. most commonly used in this book.

Making the Heddle Bar

6. Center one of the 11¾ in. (30 cm) dowels (the cloth beam) beside the 13⅝ in. (34.5 cm) dowel (this will become your heddle bar). Use the lines on the cloth beam as a guide to measure out ¼ in. (7 mm) increments in gray pencil on the heddle bar.

7. With green pencil, mark ¼ in. (7 mm) increments to sit centrally between each of the gray lines on the heddle bar. The lines should alternate along the length of the bar, as shown **(7a)**. This side is the "face" of the heddle bar. Cut into the gray pencil lines as indicated in the diagram **(7b)**, across the face of the heddle bar, the left side, and for 3⁄16 in. (5 mm) on the right and reverse sides of the bar. Repeat for the green pencil lines, this time sawing into the face of the heddle bar, the right side, and for 3⁄16 in. (5 mm) on the left and reverse sides **(7c)**. Saw each marking 3⁄16 in. (5 mm) deep and sand smooth.

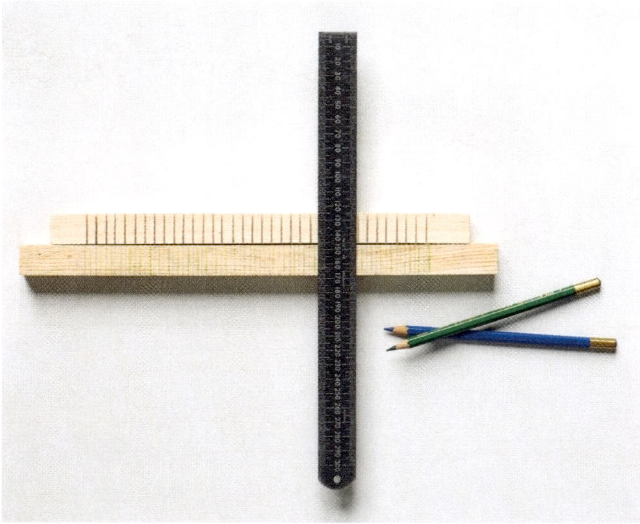

7a

DOTTED LINES INDICATE CUTS

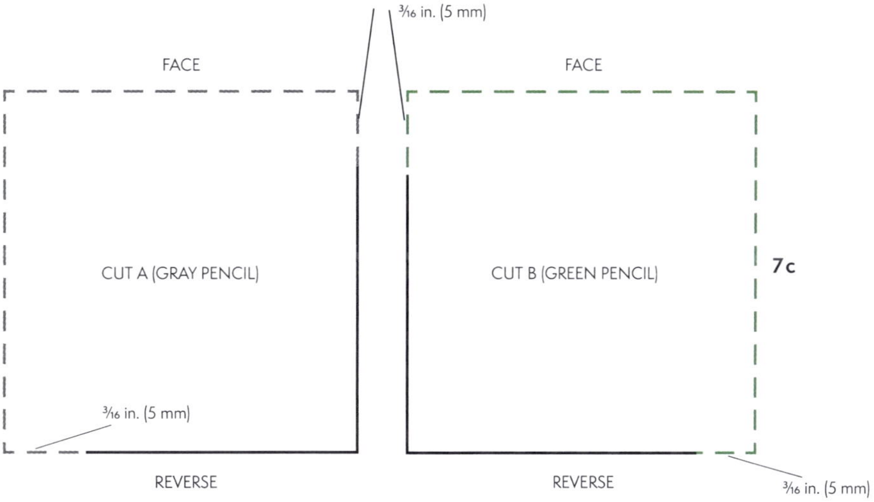

7b **7c**

8 and 9

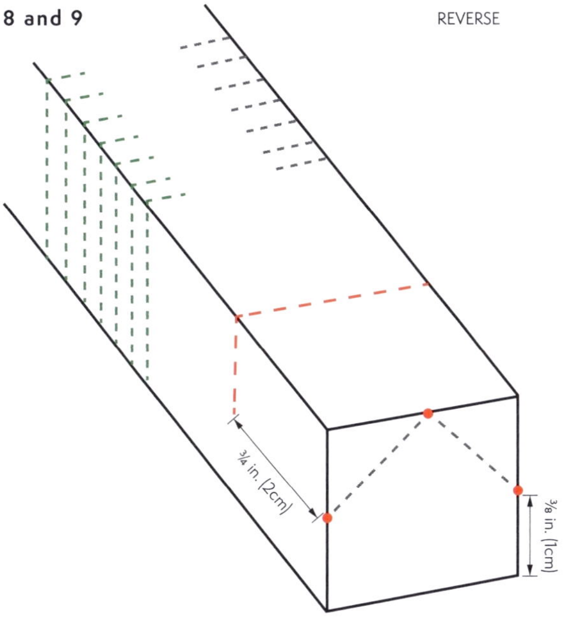

8. As the heddle bar must rock back and forth to open the warp sheds, cut the ends so that it can move easily. To begin, on the reverse side of the heddle bar, measure ¾ in. (2 cm) in from the end of the heddle bar and mark the line in pencil. Continue drawing this line on the left and right sides of the reverse side, for ⅜ in. (1 cm). Repeat for the other end of the heddle bar.

9. On each end of the bar, make a pencil mark halfway along three sides of the bar and join them to create a "house" shape.

10

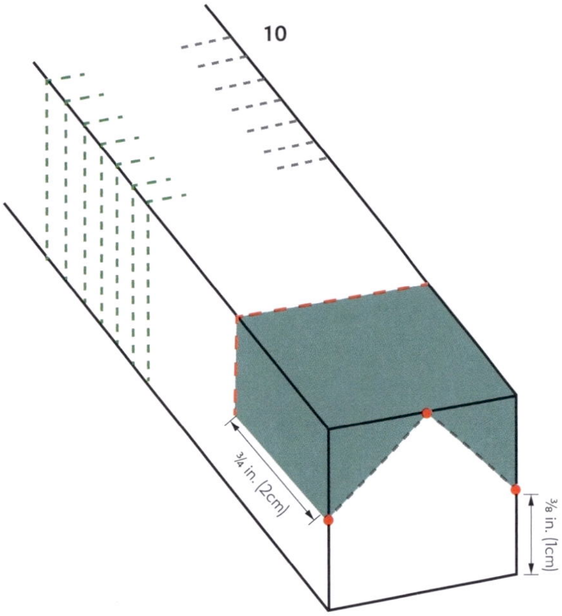

10. To begin cutting away the blue section in the diagram, saw down the diagonal lines on the end until you meet the ¾ in. (2 cm) mark.

11

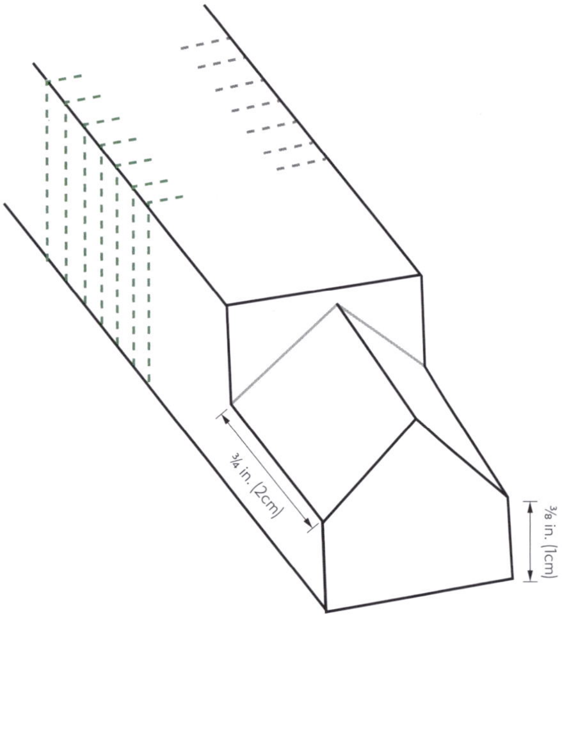

11. Saw inward from the end ⅜ in. (1 cm) lines until both cuts meet and you have created a "house" shape, as shown. Repeat on the other end of the dowel.

Assembling the Loom

12. Lay out all the frame pieces, as shown below.

13. Drill a 1½ in. (3.5 cm) hole into both ends of the cloth and warp beams. Make sure the holes are placed centrally.

14. Drill a slightly larger hole all the way through the top and bottom of the side bars, to align with the holes in the cloth and warp beams.

15. Screw the bolts into each corner (through the side bars and cloth and warp beams), until the ends of the bolts sticking out measure ¾ in. (2 cm). Put on the washers and tighten with the wing nuts.

Place the heddle bar across your new loom.

Happy weaving!

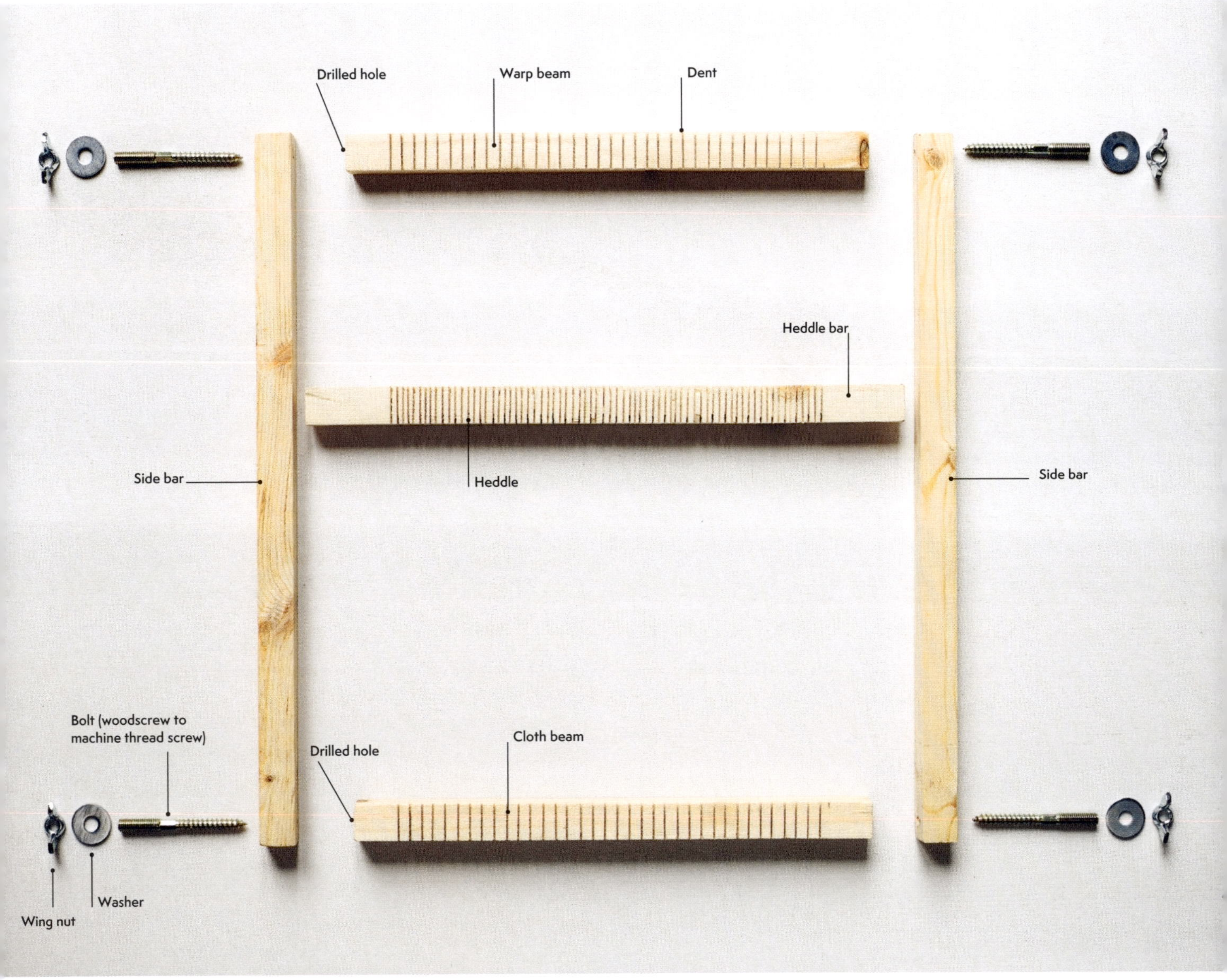

GRAFTING

Some of the projects in this book are made from more than one woven piece that you will need to join together. This grafting stitch will allow you to do this securely and almost invisibly. All you need is a darning needle—the project instructions will tell you when to stitch the pieces together and which yarn from your project to use.

1. Align the selvage of the two pieces of weaving next to each other—they will be stitched reverse sides together. You will be grafting together the corresponding pick of each piece.

2. Thread the darning needle with a length of yarn and secure the yarn with a double stitch at the beginning of your grafted selvage.

3. Starting at the bottom of the selvage on the first piece, pass the grafting yarn up through the first pick loop on the selvage, then pass it again down through the corresponding pick loop on the other selvage.

4. Continue, weaving the grafting yarn back and forth between the selvages. Gently but firmly pull the grafting yarn as you go to bring the edges together.

5. When you reach the end, secure the grafting yarn with a double stitch and tuck the tail into the weft yarns on the reverse side of the weaving.

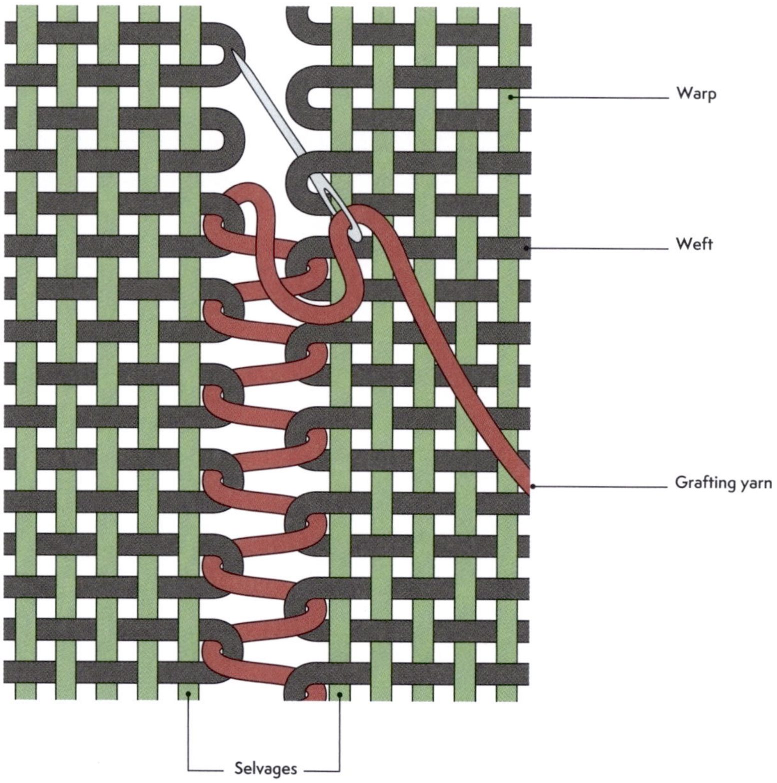

KNOTS

The following three knots are used in various techniques and projects throughout the book.

Overhand Knot

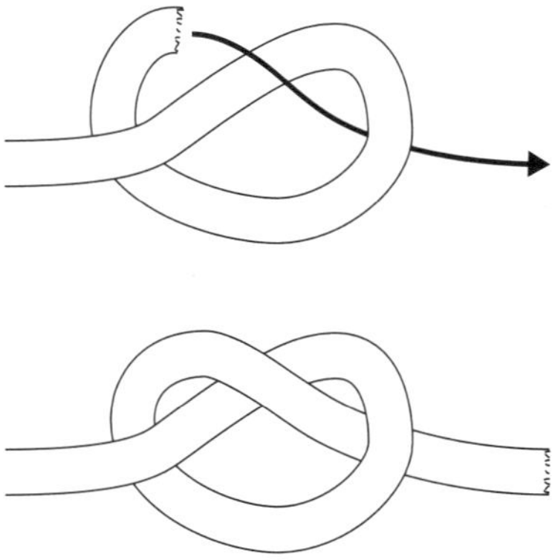

1. Take the tail end of the thread under, then over itself, sliding it through the loop you just created.

2. Pull both ends of the thread in opposite directions to tighten.

Half Hitch Knot

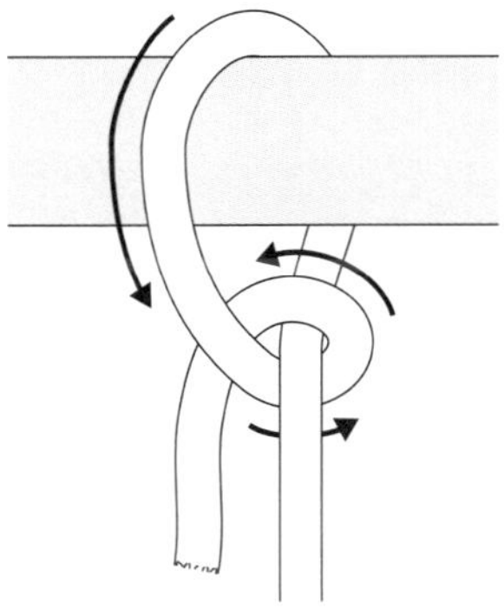

1. Wrap the thread around the object once. You now have two ends of thread—the active thread on the left and the center thread on the right. Thread the active thread under the center thread from the right and up through the opening on the left.

2. Pull the active thread tight to complete the knot.

Lark's Head Knot

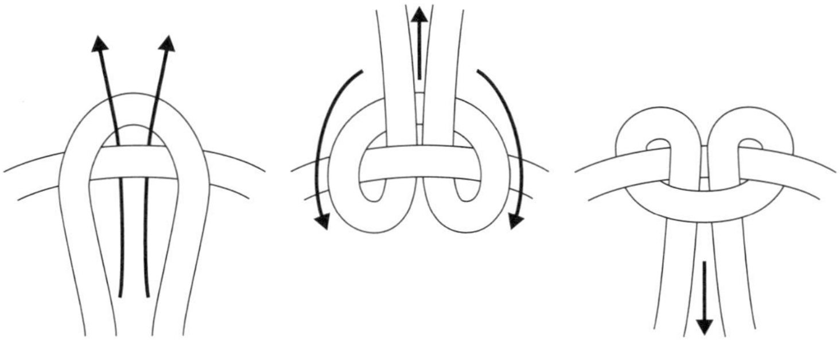

1. Start by folding the knotting thread in half to form a loop, then pass the loop under the base thread.

2. Take both tail ends of the knotting thread over the base thread and through the loop.

3. Pull to tighten.

GLOSSARY

BALANCED WEAVE
When there are the same number of warp ends as there are weft picks per the same unit of measurement.

BAST FIBER
Fiber collected from plant stems.

BEAT
Securing a pick into position using a beater. As a noun, it means the number of picks per unit of measurement.

BEATER
The implement used to beat down each weft shot after weaving (see Handweaving with a Heddle Bar, page 34). A weaving comb or a kitchen fork can be used for this task in frame loom weaving.

BLOCK
One pattern or threading unit, or one area forming a separate section. As a verb, it means to set a piece of work into shape.

BODKIN
A needle with a blunt end. Also known as a darning needle.

CLOTH BEAM
The rotating beam at the bottom of the loom (closest to the weaver), around which the woven cloth is wound and held in tension.

DENT
The space between two pegs or slits across the cloth and warp beams of a frame loom.

DRAFT
The diagrammatic representation of the threading order and weaving sequence, revealing the textile's structure.

DRESSING THE LOOM
Placing the warp onto the loom—winding, tensioning, and tying.

END
A warp thread.

EXTRA-WEFT ROW
An additional weft woven between two regular (ground) weft threads to create an ornamental pattern in addition to the ground weave.

FABRIC
Cloth, textile, or a woven piece.

FACE OF CLOTH
The top side of the fabric.

FELL
The place on the loom where the unwoven warp and last weft meet.

FIBER
The small hairlike material that is spun into yarn. May be natural or man-made.

FINISHING
The work done to the woven piece after it has been removed from the loom.

FLOAT
A length of yarn (warp or weft) that goes over more than one weft or warp.

FRINGE
The ends of the warp either left loose or grouped.

GROUND-WEFT ROWS
Weft rows, usually of plain weave or twill structure, woven between decorative extra-weft rows.

HEADING CORD
A piece of weaving to space the warp threads and provide a firm base upon which to begin weaving.

LONG HEDDLE
The set of lower dents on a heddle bar.

LOOM WASTE
The portion of the warp that cannot be woven.

MENDING
Darning loose threads and broken ends, and replacing wrong picks.

PICK
A single inserted row of weft yarn. Also known as a shot.

PLAIN WEAVE
The warp and weft interlace created by moving over and under single threads.

SELVAGE
The closed woven edge on either side of the cloth.

SETT
The number of ends per measuring unit. Also, the number of picks per unit.

SHED
The name given to the triangular space or opening between two sets of warp threads—those that are raised and those that are lowered—into which the weft is placed.

SHED STICK
A thin, broad stick inserted into the warp that can be turned on its edge to create a shed.

SHOT
See Pick.

SHRINKAGE
The reduction in length of the warp and width of the weft due to interlacement.

SHUTTLE
The stick or implement that holds the weft.

SKEIN
A length of yarn, loosely coiled and knotted.

TASSEL
A bound bunch of threads.

TEMPLE
An adjustable tool used on a loom to maintain the width and improve the edges of the woven fabric.

TENSION
The degree to which the warp and weft are stretched during weaving.

THREAD
A long, thin strand of any type of fiber used in sewing or weaving.

TWILL
Weaving a set combination of adjacent ends together by sequential raising or lowering of those combinations.

WARP
The threads stretching vertically between the cloth and warp beams of the loom. Also, the threads along the length of the cloth.

WARP BEAM
The rotating beam at the top of the loom (farthest from the weaver), around which the unwoven warp is wound and held in tension.

WARP-FACED
Weaving in which the warp threads are dominant on the surface.

WEAVE
The systematic order of interlacements of warp and weft threads.

WEFT
The yarn passing from side to side. Also, the yarns along the width of the cloth.

WEFT-FACED
Weaving in which the weft threads are dominant on the surface.

YARN
Fibers spun into thread-like form. Also, the type of thread used in most weaving projects.

INDEX

Projects are in **bold**.

ACKNOWLEDGMENTS

With thanks,

To the entire team at Quarto, to my copy editor Jen Fox-Proverbs, to my photographers Al Higgins, Nicki Dowey, and Phil Wilkins.

To all the dedicated and enthusiastic little loom weavers around the world who helped spur on the idea for this new book!

Many thanks for the yarn sponsorships from West Yorkshire Spinners, Brooklyn Tweed, UK Alpaca, Wool and the Gang, BC Garn, and Onion.

IMAGE CREDITS

Page 7: Photo by Damien McGlynn
Page 11: Photo by Julian Mora on Unsplash
Page 13: Illustration by pixpenart / Shutterstock.com
Page 14: Illustration by Galina Sinelnikova / Shutterstock.com
Page 15: Illustration by Channarong Pherngjanda / Shutterstock.com
Page 16: Illustration by Komleva / Shutterstock.com
Page 17: Illustration by Airin.dizain / Shutterstock.com